THIS I
BELIEVE

Previous books published by John Wiley & Sons in the *This I Believe* series, edited by Dan Gediman, John Gregory, and Mary Jo Gediman:

This I Believe: On Love

THIS I
BELIEVE

On Fatherhood

EDITED BY DAN GEDIMAN
WITH JOHN GREGORY
AND MARY JO GEDIMAN

JOSSEY-BASS
A Wiley Imprint
www.josseybass.com

Published by Jossey-Bass
A Wiley Imprint
989 Market Street, San Francisco, CA 94103-1741—www.josseybass.com

Design by Forty-five Degree Design, LLC.

Jossey-Bass books and products are available through most bookstores. To contact Jossey-Bass directly call our Customer Care Department within the U.S. at 800-956-7739, outside the U.S. at 317-572-3986, or fax 317-572-4002.

Jossey-Bass also publishes its books in a variety of electronic formats. Some content that appears in print may not be available in electronic books.

Library of Congress Cataloging-in-Publication Data

On fatherhood / edited by Dan Gediman ; with John Gregory and Mary Jo Gediman.
   p.   cm. — (This I believe)
ISBN 978-0-470-87647-3 (cloth); ISBN 978-1-118-02554-3 (ebk);
ISBN 978-1-118-02556-7 (ebk); ISBN 978-1-118-02557-4 (ebk)
   1. Fatherhood. 2. Fathers. I. Gediman, Dan. II. Gregory, John, date.
III. Gediman, Mary Jo.
HQ756.O53   2011
306.874'2—dc22

                                                2011002093

Printed in the United States of America
FIRST EDITION
HB Printing 10 9 8 7 6 5 4 3 2 1

To Margot Trevor Wheelock,
who was responsible for
This I Believe

CONTENTS

THIS I
BELIEVE

Introduction

Since launching *This I Believe* on public radio in 2005, we have received some 90,000 essays from men, women, and young people from all walks of life. Every day, our team reads through these essays, and we have noticed that certain themes recur time and again: love and friendship, faith and spirituality, patriotism and democracy.

The parent-child relationship looms especially large in this collection as the one relationship we all experience: we are all someone's child, and many of us are parents (either literally or symbolically) to a young person. It is a relationship that many of the world's sacred texts enjoin us to honor. It is a relationship filled with joy and heartbreak, love and anger, lessons learned, and opportunities missed.

Given how prominently paternal figures play in our culture, we decided to continue our book series with this collection on fatherhood, which we hope to follow soon with an edition on motherhood. We are excited to offer you these intimate, heartfelt views into one of our most fundamental relationships. Although relatively brief, these essays brim with memorable characters—fathers, mothers, sons, and daughters—trying to navigate life's challenges, large and small.

Under the best circumstances, fathers are a positive role model: think Atticus Finch in *To Kill a Mockingbird* or Dr. Cliff Huxtable from television's *The Cosby Show*—the honorable, dependable, loving stalwarts who teach life lessons by example and with a touch of humor. Yet at other times, the father may be more like King Lear or Willy Loman, figures so dark and troubled that their parenting skills may have no redeeming qualities. In reality, though, most of our fathers don't fit the archetypes of literature or popular culture. They are simply human—men trying above all else to live up to the enormous expectations that their families, modern society, and their own aspirations place on them.

Regardless of the nature of the filial bond, the father-child relationship offers innumerable opportunities for both parties to learn, and grow, and form belief.

In this book, you'll read reflections from expectant dads, full of optimism and prebirth jitters, as well as from long-time parents who, through the distance of time, are able to reflect on their successes and failures as fathers. We also hear from and about adoptive fathers, single dads, step-fathers, and men who volunteer to fill the shoes of absent fathers.

You'll also read essays from children (some young and some well into adulthood) writing about their fathers. They honestly and openly introduce us to the men who shaped them, sometimes in surprising ways. They talk about the fathers they want to emulate, the mistakes they hope to avoid repeating, and the wisdom they realized they gained.

"So, you're creating a guidebook for being a good father," one person said upon hearing about this collection of essays. In a way, perhaps we are. There are certainly valuable insights to be gleaned from these essays that could benefit new or soon-to-be dads. But more than that, we see this book as an invitation to reflect on the give-and-take in any relationship between an elder and a younger person—that there are opportunities for both parties to love and to grow.

We hear the wisdom and acceptance that comes with time, of children who mature enough to finally hear the message from Dad, and of fathers who finally embrace the child as he or she truly is. Sometimes the life lessons are written down, such as the police officer with a letter tucked in his locker with instructions to give it to his children in case of his death. Other times, the lessons are spoken, as when a father lectures his son on how to deal with a racist remark. Sometimes they are delivered on a basketball court, in a garden, or at the barbershop.

Taken as a whole, these stories of fathers and their children remind us that life's most mundane moments— changing diapers, mowing the lawn, casting for fish, pondering the existence of Santa Claus—can reveal deeper, richer insights if we're quiet enough and patient enough to discover them.

Truth and the Santa Claus Moment

COREY HARBAUGH

I believe our lives are condensed into moments like this one: my son Tucker approached me at the grill where I was focused on fire and dinner, unaware that his eight-year-old mind was struggling for the right words to fit around a question. Finally, he spoke: "Dad, if I asked you if it was you who bought presents at Christmas instead of Santa, would you tell me?"

I heard questions within questions: is there a Santa Claus, what is Christmas if there isn't, and, most important, can I trust you to tell me the truth, Dad? At the heart of each question I heard my son asking if he could still believe what he had believed all his life.

I couldn't answer him just then because his six-year-old sister and five-year-old, soon-to-be stepbrother were playing nearby in the yard, and also because I couldn't turn from the grill to look fully into his eyes like I wanted to for as long as it took both of us to understand.

How we answer these questions matters, and though we spend hours and days and weeks and years trying to figure out the answers, we only get to live them out in small moments. This was one of those moments, for both of us.

All of my life I have tried to put words around the questions about what I believe, and have found that the answers to my biggest questions have no words. They have moments. Like noticing the nun who wept while she prayed in St. Peter's, an island of quiet faith surrounded by a sea of noisy tourists. Like the upwelling of pride and fear when my daughter took to her bike the first time, her legs pumping her steady, and steadily away from me. Like burying my grandfather on the same day my son was born. Like sitting around the coffee table with my children and their mother two years prior, watching their faces come short of comprehending the word "divorce."

That night after dinner I took Tuck for a bike ride, and we sat on a grassy hill drinking a soda, watching the orange sun sink behind a line of trees. I brought up his question from the grill. "Tuck, earlier you asked me about Santa."

He stopped me. "Don't answer me, Dad. I think I know the answer, and right now I just want something to believe in."

I turned to my son and was able to finally look into his big eyes. "Tucker, your question was if you asked me about Santa, would I tell you, and my answer is yes. If you ask, I will tell you."

He considered this a moment, smiled, and before he drank the last swallow of soda pop he told me easily, "Then I'm not going to ask."

That was good enough for both of us. For now. There will be other questions like this to come, no doubt. They, too, will have their moments.

COREY HARBAUGH lives in Gobles, Michigan, and teaches English at the local high school. As a member of the Third Coast Writing Project, Mr. Harbaugh promotes the power of writing in the National Writing Project network. He and his wife are raising four children in a healthy, busy blended family.

The Last Harvest

RANDI PERKINS

My dad, Robert W. "Bud" Perkins, grew up on a farm homesteaded by his father in southwestern North Dakota. Except for a year in Los Angeles in 1940 working for Douglas Aircraft, he spent his entire life on that farm. Surviving the 1920s and '30s gave him a tremendous work ethic and will to succeed.

As I was growing up, I assumed my dad had many dreams and goals that he never had the chance to pursue. I imagined he saw farming as the only thing he knew or was qualified to do. After having a family, Dad resigned himself to remaining there on the farm, making a living and supporting his wife and children. He was just trying to do "the right thing."

I grew up on that farm, and when I was old enough, I worked in those fields with Dad. But I wasn't very mechanically inclined and never liked to get my hands dirty, so I couldn't see myself becoming a farmer. From an early age, I wrote and performed songs. I played in rock bands during summer breaks from college. Music became my true passion, the dream I had to follow.

But growing up in North Dakota, the music business was only a distant vision, not something to make a living doing. I felt the prevailing wisdom, "the right thing," was to follow a career where I could be easily employed and make a good living. I became a certified public accountant with a master of business administration degree. I moved to the city, and tried many different jobs, hoping to one day make enough money to spend time writing songs and getting into the music business. After twenty years of career and financial disappointments, I realized I could never attain my musical goals that way, nor would I ever make any money.

In October 2000, my dad retired from farming and sold the machinery he no longer needed. I attended the auction to see one last time that farm and equipment I had worked on as a kid. I saw my dad as a successful and contented farmer who, after setting aside his other dreams and goals, managed to overcome the hardships of agriculture and become a well-respected man in his hometown.

After an emotional day of watching people buy and take his machinery, I decided to ask my dad, "If you could start all over and follow your dream, what would it be?"

Without hesitation my dad said, "Farming *was* my dream."

Since that sunny autumn day, my life has never been the same. At that moment I realized the example my dad set for me wasn't what I thought. He did "the right thing" by following his dream of farming.

Now I know I have to follow the passion in my heart for music. Embracing my true calling has given me a humbling sense of responsibility to be more aware of the legacy I am leaving my son and the generations that will follow him. Like my father did for me, I believe I must set an example of living my dreams.

RANDI PERKINS is an inspirational folk singer–songwriter living in Nashville, Tennessee. He composes songs and stories about family and friends, celebrating life, and growing up on a farm on the Great Plains in North Dakota.

The Dads We Were Given

KATHY WELLS MCMENAMIN

I believe in my dad. He did not contribute physically to my creation. I was adopted when I was three months old. He did not want me at first. He told my mom he was not comfortable taking on somebody else's kid. He felt tremendous guilt because a genetic condition rendered him sterile and unable to give my mother the children they both so deeply desired.

My dad was not a highly educated man. He finished high school and apprenticed in a machine shop at the Washington Navy Yard. When I was in elementary school he transferred to the Goddard Space Flight Center where he made parts for the moon buggy and the Hubble space telescope.

He was a hard worker and, after the idea of being an adoptive father took root, a great dad.

My dad chatted with everyone, a trait that caused me great embarrassment when I was a teenager. He would strike up conversations in line at the grocery store, in the seats at the movie theater, and at all the campgrounds we ever frequented. Once, while we were visiting a small airport, my dad talked a local pilot into giving me a ride in his airplane. I am amazed that he trusted a complete stranger enough to let me go, but he did. He never said "no" when I tested my own wings, whether somersaulting on the front lawn or taking off in the family station wagon to go to college four states away.

My dad saved lives. Once while swimming in a lake in Iowa, he rescued a drowning boy. To my dad it wasn't a "big deal"—it was just what you did. Then there was the time our next-door neighbor's house caught fire. My brother (who is also adopted) saw the flames and woke my dad to tell him. Dad told my mom to call the fire department and then he went next door to help. He opened the front door and called out. Our neighbor answered but he could not see her because of the thick smoke. So Dad stretched out on the floor with his feet hooked on the doorframe and kept calling to her to come toward his voice. Eventually he felt her hand and pulled her out of the burning, smoke-filled home. He stayed to assist the firemen when they came and only after my mom pointed out that he was only wearing his skivvies did he go home.

My dad fixed things. He fixed the car when it broke down. He repaired the hot water heater when it stopped making hot water. He kissed skinned knees and mended the skateboards that caused them. I don't remember anything he couldn't fix except maybe his own appetite for good food, and the brain-stem stroke that took him in his sixty-fourth year.

As I said good-bye to my dad in the Neurology ICU, I told him that I loved him. I told him that I didn't need to find my "real parents" because he and Mom were my *real* parents. I thanked him for being my dad.

I believe, sometimes, the best dads are the ones we are given.

KATHY WELLS MCMENAMIN lives in Lafayette, Colorado, with her husband, Mike, and their two daughters. At her mother's urging, Ms. McMenamin researched her biological parents' health history. She learned that her biological father, who had reluctantly relinquished her at birth, died in a car accident in 1983. His family told Ms. McMenamin that he had carried her baby picture in his wallet for years. She considers herself lucky to have had two amazing fathers.

Forgiving My Dad

BRYAN MCGUIRE

I believe in the power of forgiveness.

I never really understood what forgiveness meant. When I felt treated badly, it seemed natural to hold on tightly to the anger and resentment.

I never expressed anger outwardly. Instead, I let it stew. My righteous indignation toward those who hurt me was a shield from my pain. Most of this indignation was directed at my father. I blamed Dad for everything bad that happened to me.

Over the years, his misdeeds and shortcomings became the scapegoat for my own. The fact that I hadn't become an alcoholic like him was justification for being irresponsible, dishonest, and thoughtless.

Throughout years of struggle, dysfunctional relationships, and little to no career advancement, I never took responsibility for anything. I laid all my troubles on Dad.

Then a few years ago, something shocking happened to me: I became a father.

One night, as I watched my newborn son sleep, studying his beautiful face, I suddenly became filled with fear. I was convinced I would screw him up—that all my problems would wash over him, tarnishing his perfect soul. Strangely, while panicking about my son's impending doom, Dad popped to mind.

I sat there in the dark, surrounded by the soothing sounds and smells of my baby's room, and I thought of how Dad must have felt when I was born. I knew at that moment that he never intended to hurt me. I realized that he loved me just as I loved my son. I knew that he had done the best he could, even if it wasn't always very good.

I forgave my father that night—for all the times he got drunk, embarrassed me, or hurt my mother. I forgave him for not being around. I let go of the resentment I'd held toward him for so many years. I stopped blaming him.

Maybe my reasons were not very noble. Maybe I was afraid my son would blame me for whatever problems would inevitably fall his way. But whatever the reason, for the first time, I saw my dad as a real person. I knew he didn't drink to hurt me. He drank because he was flawed and hurting. I knew that if I didn't forgive him, I would never have the kind of relationship I wanted with my son. If I kept blaming him I would never start living my life.

Dad hadn't asked for my forgiveness; he's never acknowledged that he's done anything wrong. But I realized that in forgiving him, what I was really doing was taking responsibility for myself and my own actions.

Forgiving my dad changed my life. I accepted him for who he was and that set me free. My eyes are open now to my own failings. And I discovered that forgiving someone is both an innately spiritual act that brings us closer to a higher power, and a uniquely human act that connects people in a way that strengthens us all. It is a powerful thing. This I believe.

BRYAN MCGUIRE is a marketing administrator in Chicago, Illinois, where he lives with his wife and three children. He recently completed his master's degree in counseling psychology and hopes to one day work with individuals and families coping with alcoholism and drug abuse.

·

Appreciating the Moment

JAY HASHEIDER

Moving away from home is both a good and a sad thing. It is every child's and every parent's goal to eventually achieve separation, but it is nevertheless sad when it happens. So it was with heavy hearts on a Sunday in August that my son and I worked to prepare his car for a milestone journey—the day he moved across the country after twenty years of living under my roof.

We started early, but our work went slowly into the afternoon. The Sunday baseball game came on. Our hometown Cardinals were playing the Atlanta Braves.

I overheard bits of the TV broadcast—Atlanta took a two-run lead as we were packing the trunk. The score stayed the same as we fixed snacks for his trip. After that I became absorbed in glum thoughts about his departure and completely forgot about the game. I was stuffing the back seat with the last items when I heard the door open. "Dad," he said, "come on in. Let's watch the rest of the game. They're only down by a run."

His red-colored eyes instantly told me that he, too, found this to be a difficult passage and that he, too, wanted to share one last father-son moment. Without hesitation I led the way to the TV set. There, we found the game in the ninth inning with the Cards still losing 3–1. "Oh," he said, "they're down two runs. Never mind." His voice cracked with doubt. "I thought they were coming back."

"That's fine," I said, wanting so much to stretch this last moment before he left. "Let's watch anyway."

The Cards got to bat last. First a single, then another, followed by an infield hit that loaded the bases. Suddenly the game became very interesting. As David Eckstein walked up to the plate with one out, the drama of the game took us over. The sadness of that day was replaced momentarily by watching an exciting baseball game, something we had done many times together before.

That's when the magic moment came. When David Eckstein parked the third pitch into the seats. It was a come-from-behind, walk-off, grand-slam home run, only his fifth home run of the season.

In that one moment we were transformed, ecstatically jumping up and down and experiencing a joy that I could never imagine happening on that bittersweet afternoon. It was a wonderful feeling that made the day, the trip, our life, seem so right.

And then he left.

I believe in magical moments that happen when I least expect them. The joy—amidst the sadness—that we both experienced that afternoon was a gift, a divine presence. Such moments cannot be planned, or even hoped for. They are gifts that appear and then disappear, just like my son as he drove off that afternoon to start a new chapter in his life.

JAY HASHEIDER is the proud father of stepdaughter, Gymi Renee, and son, Nick. He loves numbers and is delighted to share the same birth date with his son—and fellow Missourian Mark Twain. Mr. Hasheider also shares Mark Twain's outlook on life: "Obscurity and competence. That is the life that is best worth living."

Whistling in the Light

T. A. BARRON

On the day my dad died, I felt numb. He had dealt with cancer for several years, so I thought I was ready.

But I wasn't.

When I came home that day, the screen door banged closed behind me. I noticed that our three normally rambunctious kids were very, very quiet. And I thought about the feel of my dad's hand inside my own—how warm it was, even at the end.

We all sat down at the kitchen table and started to dig into a platter of cold spaghetti. Everyone stayed quiet, for quite some time. Then my five-year-old daughter broke the silence with a question: "Hey, do you want to know my most favorite time with Grandpa?"

Still numb, I only half heard what she said, but I managed a nod. She then described how he had taken her for a walk on his Colorado ranch and shown her his special sitting stone down by the creek. As she spoke about that experience, I remembered how that same man had taken me on that same walk when I was just her age.

Then her younger brothers joined in with their favorite times—and before long, the air around our kitchen table was absolutely filled with memories of that man I was missing. All of their stories took place out in nature, where he loved to be, whatever the season. And very slowly, my numbness started to melt away.

Finally, I told a story of my own—how, as a kid, I'd gone outside with my dad on one of those clear Colorado nights when the stars are so bright you almost have to squint just to look at them. I remembered feeling, under those stars, both very small and very large, at once—both humbled by my own insignificance and magnified by my own connection to the grand sweep of creation. As we stood there, looking up, my dad started to whistle, sending his lonely, lilting notes skyward. And I wondered if the stars might ever whistle back, joining in a celestial chorus.

All at once, at our kitchen table, I realized that maybe my dad wasn't so far away after all. I still missed him, of course, just as I do now. But thanks to the wisdom of my children, I had a good idea where to find him.

I believe in the enduring power of love, which stays with us long after our loved ones have departed. And I believe in the healing power of nature, which inspires us in wondrous ways.

After supper, I went outside, looked up at the stars—and listened.

T. A. BARRON grew up in Colorado ranch country and traveled widely as a Rhodes Scholar. His highly acclaimed, internationally best-selling books include *The Lost Years of Merlin*, *The Ancient One*, and *The Hero's Trail*, plus nature books about Colorado wilderness. Founder of a national prize for heroic kids, he loves to write and hike—and also whistle.

Lingering at the Doors

~

JOHN WARLEY

When my four children were younger, I relished one ritual above all others. Hours after their bedtime and often after mine, I walked down the carpeted hallway dividing their rooms. I walked barefoot, as soundless as a cat; silence reinforced the intimacy of the ritual. I paused briefly at each door. I didn't open it. I just stood there, thinking about the child inside, and about how if I opened the door, I'd find a son or my daughter asleep in their favorite position, clothes or toys or books or stuffed animals or soccer shin guards strewn all about depending on whose room it happened to be. It wasn't important for me to actually see that scene. I'd seen it often enough when I told them goodnight.

But there was a time, a couple of years before, when I couldn't tell them goodnight because my wife and I had separated. During the year apart, I stayed at a friend's summer home. I walked the wooden floors there, my footsteps echoing in the hollow hallway. I tried to hang a couple of pictures on the wall of my room, but they didn't belong in that place, and neither did I.

During that long, difficult year, my wife and I stayed in touch and sought counseling. When we finally reunited, my nocturnal trips down the carpeted hall began. It was only important that I knew they were in there, as safe as an enclosed room in a suburb could make them and sure to wake the next morning. No doubt some of the feeling that came over me during these forays was linked to my role as guardian, the high sheriff of 4 Deans Circle. If a fire broke out, I would evacuate them. If an intruder entered, I would confront him. If a Biblical thunderstorm shook the house, those still too young to sleep through it could take refuge in our king-size bed at the end of the hall.

I knew that this span of years (the oldest was thirteen and the youngest, six) would be meteorically brief. Soon one would be driving, then another, out on the highway, where I had no control over them or anyone else, a high sheriff with no badge who waited for *the* call that mercifully never came. But when I took these midnight strolls, those years of anxiety were still in the future, a fact that enabled me to savor the moment outside each door because I knew they were all there, all four, safe and protected.

In December my wife and I will celebrate our thirty-ninth anniversary. We rarely talk about those dark days, and when we do, we express our mutual and profound joy that we were able to reconcile. Our youngest turned thirty this year. Grandchildren populate family photos. The kids seem happy and productive. My fear of an empty hall is long past, and I believe in the moments I lingered outside each door, reminding myself that it is not just fire, or storms, or highways that can harm a child.

JOHN WARLEY is a Virginia attorney. In the 1990s he spent two years in San Miguel de Allende, Mexico, where he completed a novel and taught U.S. business law at the Tecnológico de Monterrey. He and his wife, Barbara, spend most of their time in Beaufort, South Carolina, enjoying the sunsets from their boat.

A Love Beyond Boundaries

BRIAN SCHOENI

I believe in adoption. You don't need a PhD to figure that out when you see my family.

My wife and I are average-looking Caucasians. According to our daughters' homeland, I have big a nose. They, on the other hand, have small noses. Not to mention dancing almond eyes that are black—unless you get up close and look at them in bright sunshine—and black hair that is hot to the touch as it soaks up the Colorado sun.

Yes, we are from America's middle; they are from China's. But the geographies of land and face are irrelevant.

I believe in adoption because of its intentionality; because of how it changes lives; because of the way it puts skin and bones, laughter and tears on the whole idea of hope.

My wife and I knew we'd have kids. When we finally got serious about it, all roads led back to adoption. We adopted because we wanted to. Or maybe we did it because we were supposed to.

But make no mistake: our parenthood is anything but unplanned. We did paperwork. We worked extra jobs to pay agency fees. And we waited.

And then, a day that started with a sewage backup in our master bathroom ended with an e-mail delivering the most amazing JPEG: a wide-eyed girl wearing multiple sweaters, her hair tied up in a topknot with red, white, and pink ribbons. Our daughter.

I printed out that photo and carried it everywhere, including to the other side of the world, where I got to hold the real thing, and realize just how big—and small— the world really is.

Sometimes people—usually strangers who see us out and about—act like my wife and I are on track for sainthood because we've adopted three girls who, by no fault of their own, found themselves navigating life without a family.

Those people don't get it. Adoption is not about me and my kids. It's about all of us.

It's about taking something that in some ways is selfish—wanting to be a parent—and transforming it into something that affirms the best in humanity: the ability to love someone unconditionally, simply because I choose to.

I am not alone. Families that grow by way of adoption are everywhere, and we defy stereotypes. I'm not old. I'm not infertile. I'm not driven by pity or piety. I'm just a guy who knows I'm the luckiest dad in the world.

I wish that adopting was on everyone's radar. Not as some peripheral blip, some second-choice backup plan, but as part of that very first "should-we-become-parents?" conversation.

I know adoption isn't a perfect fit for every parent-to-be. But I do believe this: adoption is a perfect fit for every kid in every corner of our world who needs the love of a family.

BRIAN SCHOENI is a dad, husband, and journalist who lives in the Denver, Colorado, area with his wife and their three daughters.

Hunting Pennies

JAMES PFREHM

From across the parking lot he looks like an old man with one too many screws loose: eyes fixed on the blacktop, shuffling in an aimless wander, halting now and then to bend over and examine the pavement more closely. From afar it is, perhaps, hard to imagine that this quirky old man has inspired my personal belief.

I call him Dad, and because of him I believe in hunting for pennies.

Some years ago I tagged along when our car needed service. "About an hour," the mechanic told us.

"Not a problem," my father said and pointed. "We'll be across the way." I followed him outside and across the street to a Denny's parking lot. It was early on a Saturday morning and the lot was still largely empty.

"I'm going to get strawberry pancakes with whipped cream," I said as we approached the entrance. But when I turned around, my dad wasn't behind me; he was stooped over in the parking lot.

"The first find of the morning," he announced, holding up his prize: a grimy, dull penny.

For the next hour we combed the asphalt for coins. Some, my father narrated, were purposefully discarded. Others were the result of hasty patrons yanking their keys from change-filled pockets. Either way, he explained, their loss would be our gain.

Though I wasn't exactly won over by his rationale for standing around for an hour, hungry and tired, hoping to pocket a few cents, I indulged the Old Man. So began our tradition: every time we were stuck with a wait, my father and I would go hunting for abandoned coins.

I only recently started to consider the larger picture of our ritual. Although we weren't rich, my parents' hard work had provided our family with what I would now call a comfortable upper-middle-class existence. It wasn't like my dad needed to pick up random coins. Why, then, waste time looking for something we didn't need? The answers

I've come up with form the foundation of my personal philosophy.

First, be active. Instead of loafing in a waiting room, get up and move around. Like many Americans, there's a history of heart attacks in my family. The less I sit around, the better it is for my ticker.

Second, keep an eye out for opportunity. I'd rather be one cent richer than one cent poorer; and it's not going to happen unless I pay attention.

Third, have a goal. No matter how small, set your mind to it. Success doesn't come without commitment.

Finally, don't be too quick to judge. Sure, that old codger in the parking lot may look like an escapee from the local loony bin, but remember: he just might be the one who found that twenty-dollar bill you swore was in the left-front pocket of your jeans.

There are a lot of abandoned pennies out there. I believe each of us owes it to ourselves to keep a look out for them.

JAMES PFREHM is a professor of German and linguistics in Ithaca, New York, where he lives with his two wiener dogs, Frida and Diego. On a Saturday morning you can still find him (and his dogs) scanning empty parking lots for abandoned coins.

A Mark in History

ROSITA CHOY

As an Asian American immigrant, I grew up in the living quarters above a small corner grocery store in East Los Angeles, believing that my purpose in life was to make a mark in history. My parents worked downstairs and lived a kind of life deferred—all their dreams and desires suspended in the present to be realized in the future, through their children. My parents and I had immigrated to the United States when I was a year old. I felt a heavy responsibility to make something of myself to repay them for their sacrifice. And my goal had to extend beyond mortality.

My father didn't speak much about his past. Upon our arrival to the United States, he bought that small corner store in East L.A. and tended to it with my mother until he retired two decades later. It was only when I began thinking of college that he told me he had a bachelor's degree in economics. A chance encounter with a mail-order catalog was the first time I heard the word "rattan" and learned that my father had once been in the import-export business in Hong Kong.

When he found me staying up late one night reading a novel, he explained that he had done the same as a youth, had begun a literary magazine, and had translated books from Russian to Chinese. An article I wrote for school led him to mention his reporting from the front lines of World War II. Finally, during one visit home after college, I asked him to tell me his entire life's story completely and chronologically so that I could thread together the anecdotes to write his story.

As I grew up, I learned that no matter how important one's deeds or ideas, they would not be a part of history if they were not written down. I became fixated on recording my father's history when I discovered that he hadn't always lived a quiet, unremarkable life.

My father died several years ago, and I have yet to begin to write his life. At the funeral and during the days after, friends and family expressed more than polite sympathy.

Their grief rose from genuine fondness. I realized that old-time customers from his corner store did not love my father because of his learnedness or past accomplishments. They loved him because he always smiled, asked them in Spanish about their lives, and offered them credit without questions or interest until the next paycheck. Family and friends loved him for his quiet interest in their lives and unconditional support. With my father, what you saw was what you got: a gentle, upstanding man with one big smile. That was his mark in history.

I gave the eulogy at my father's funeral. In some ways, I'd been preparing it for most of my life. After the service, a family friend said to me, "Your father was a good man. His influence can be seen in the person you've become." It was at that moment that I lost my obsession with making a mark in history and repaying my parents' hard work. At that moment, I began to believe that my true purpose in life is to have at least one person say about me, as so many have said about my father, "I knew her, and my life is a little better for having known her."

I finally understand that as long as I live my life with this belief, that will be repayment enough for my father.

ROSITA CHOY taught bilingual kindergarten for three years in the Oakland, California, public school system. She then spent the next eleven years in Oakland, Boston, and Washington, DC, working for nonprofit organizations concerned with immigrants' rights, human rights, and women's rights. Currently, she lives in Vermont with her partner.

Trimming

AMY ROWLAND

My dad is a retired barber, and much of his job involved trimming. It is delicate work to coax a blade around a man's ears, but that is what he did, six days a week, and so he sent four children to college on forty years' worth of haircuts.

I remember the shop's smell, the bottles of blue Barbicide and gold Lucky Tiger, the snap of the pinstripe barber cape, and the sound of the stiff brush whisking talc around men's necks as they stretched toward the scratch.

"Make me look decent," a country man in town shoes would say as he eased into the chair.

My dad was like the stage manager of *Our Town*—listening close and revealing little—because talking was the main activity among the men in the shop. They would sit in the row of orange chairs along the wall and wait their turn, talking all the while.

Sometimes my mother would come home with a big piece of small-town news only to discover that my dad had already heard it at the barbershop. Southern women are often accused of being gossips, but listening to men in a barbershop is like watching long-deprived pyromaniacs take a blowtorch to a drought-parched hayfield.

I learned a lot of valuable lessons from watching my dad cut hair. I learned about holding still, being respectful, paying attention, and cleaning things up. I learned not to waste words—or anything else. Often, my dad saved the hair he cut to spread around his tomato plants, not to keep the deer away or to warm the roots but because, he said, "It's protein."

I also learned about the sacredness of small acts. Dad was a deacon and then an elder in his church and sometimes would be called on to both cut hair and give communion to a man on his deathbed. To witness this intimacy between proudly masculine men, one of the final physical exchanges of a man's life, was to see grooming, like communion, as a ritual of dignity.

I wonder if I have followed in my dad's footsteps with a career of cutting away. I am a copyeditor for a newspaper index. I trim articles into short summaries. Then, I consider whether the summary itself can be trimmed. It's not the same as tracing a blade around a man's ear, and yet, it is the same idea of starting with clippers and finishing with tweezers.

So I believe in trimming.

Perhaps I have become too attached to the act of trimming. I now have the alarming experience of working on a novel that continues to get shorter as I write it. Perhaps soon I'll discover that for the past several years what I've really been writing is a mediocre haiku. Then I will just shred the other pages and give it to my dad to spread around his tomato plants.

AMY ROWLAND is a former editor for the *New York Times Index*. She was a 2009 Norman Mailer fellow, and her nonfiction has appeared in the *New York Times* and the *Smart Set*.

A Father Is Born from Many Strangers

MICHELE WELDON

My late father was a prince of a man, unapologetic for deceiving all six of his children into believing each one was his favorite. I expected nothing less for my three sons than to be adored by their father.

This was not to be.

My former husband's disappearance played out incrementally over the last fifteen years since our divorce. Now it is complete; he has vanished. A phantom parent living overseas, he has no contact with our sons, now aged twenty-one, nineteen, and sixteen.

Over time, my fury about their paternal loss has cooled. The anger that once felt flammable has been replaced by a sense of gratitude to a number of gentle and forthright men who willingly elect to take part in the lives of my boys.

I believe a father is born from many strangers.

My oldest son had two English teachers who guided him and his pinballing emotions through middle and high school. But it is his beloved high school wrestling coach who has been his fervent mentor and life guide. Between push-ups and takedowns, Coach Mike Powell offered my son his heart and earned his trust, a gift he is reluctant to share. Now in college, my son still calls Coach Powell with good news before he calls me.

For my middle son there is not only this same wrestling coach, but a cast of uncles whom he respects, admires, and emulates. He will listen to my brother Paul when my words are no longer heard. It is Uncle Mike, my sister's husband, who helps him with his chemistry and takes him on long walks. For a time Uncle Mark, their father's brother, appeared at tournaments and football games to cheer for each nephew. Two years in a row, he drove 150 miles to the state tournament to see my oldest wrestle.

My youngest found a youth football coach he imitates and respects. "I want Coach Tim to be my dad," he announced midseason of seventh grade. Though I explained that his coach had his own family, he countered that Tim was exactly the kind of man he would want as a father—funny, affectionate, tough, and in possession of his own Super Bowl ring. But now my youngest son is wrestling as well, and Coach Powell has once again moved to the dominant spot of influence.

It is not just teachers, coaches, and uncles who populate this volunteer father club, but also men like the friend who once quietly left a $50 bill in the pocket of the blue cashmere overcoat he gave my oldest to wear to a formal dance.

As their mother working fervently to answer their needs, I frequently feel overwhelmed with what I must do to ensure I raise these men well. I am charged with lassoing their strong wills so they can know success without being derailed by youthful mistakes. Relief from my panic arrives with every gesture of goodwill from these generous souls.

No one fills the shoes of a father. But the footprint that the man who fathered them left behind does not have to stay empty. I find it a profound act of selflessness that each of these men has chosen my sons, and a blessing that my sons have chosen them. In some ways, this is my boys' declaration of independence from abandonment. These men who are not required to care—but do—convince my sons they are worthy of being loved.

MICHELE WELDON is a single mother of three sons in Chicago. She is an assistant professor at Northwestern University's Medill School of Journalism and is the author of several nonfiction books. A journalist for more than thirty-two years, Ms. Weldon leads writing workshops around the country and speaks on issues related to media and women.

The Cards Will Hear You

$\backsim$

ERIC LARSON

The cards will hear you," my dad would say, when we played crazy eights or canasta on those winter nights in Minnesota, when I was young. Mom and Dad and I would play, sometimes with my sister, upstairs on the orange shag rug in the study, near the hot radiator that kept the little room warmer and cozier than the open dining room, living room, and kitchen downstairs. I hated to lose, or even to almost win. I would throw the cards and storm out when I didn't win the trick, or when I didn't get the right card.

"Don't complain! The cards will hear you," Dad would say. Apparently cards don't like complainers. Then Dad would put on this self-righteous demeanor, virtually say a prayer for the card he wanted, and say some staged gracious remark regardless of outcome. "This is a wonderful, wonderful card. I am so grateful to receive this new opportunity." If he would lose, he would say words of thanks, but playfully, and if he won, he was intolerably overbearing. "See what I mean?" he'd say. Mom would roll her eyes or slap him.

Thirty years later, I know the cards can't hear me, and no one ever believed they could. As a math professor, Dad's faith was in statistics, not prayers to the card gods. As a lawyer, I'm not taking up the case for cards having ears. But at the same time, Dad was on to something.

I believe in the power of a positive attitude, to transform fear into joy, despair into victory. To complain is to fail at the outset. A positive attitude guarantees success.

Cathedrals and castles are built, charities are funded, victories are won, conflicts are resolved, lives are lived, and cards are played—if done well—not out of fear, dread, or frustration, but out of hope and joy and an unwavering belief in success.

I recently visited my frail, eighty-nine-year-old great-great uncle in a hospital where he was recovering from a stroke, and he gave me the "squeeze 'til it hurts" handshake. "Feel this," he said, as he tried to make my hand hurt. "Ouch," I said. He showed me his flat, bony, old-man bicep—"Not too bad, is it?" He would not be defeated by a stroke or old age. This was no deathbed.

Now I play games with my children. The basement family room is vibrant, cluttered with toys, cozy, and warm, with my nine-year-old intensely transfixed at the game table and my six-year-old trying to hold the cards while playing tug-of-war with the dog. Tension rises and falls. When someone almost wins, which is often, my kids are vindictive, envious, rude, hurtful. They cry or strike out when they lose, and they gloat when they win. They behave just like children.

And I am now my dad. My wife groans or slaps me when I pass on the faith, dripping with smug resolution, but deeply in earnest: "Don't complain, and be grateful for what you have." "Remember to have fun." "The cards will hear you."

It is the most important lesson I can teach.

ERIC LARSON is a shareholder in a law firm, practicing municipal law in the greater Milwaukee area of southeast Wisconsin. He draws inspiration from his wife, who teaches at the local university, from his talented kids, and from service to local charities. He walks Toby, the family Tibetan Terrier, to and from work every day, to guarantee a happy reception at both ends.

Finding a Different Way

～

BOB MAY

Dads who have special-needs children understand that even small accomplishments mean a lot. We've learned to respect people who work extra hard to do simple things, like learning to tie shoes.

My eight-year-old son, Brian, wanted to earn a Cub Scout merit badge by learning to tie his own shoes. He was given a week to accomplish this goal. Because Brian has Down syndrome, our whole family participated, working tirelessly to teach him the knotty art of "tie-man-ship." Strangers found Brian squatting at knee level studying their shoes. While watching TV, he honed in on foot scenes, squinting for hints. Days passed and he could not seem to master it. We started to worry that he might miss the deadline. He became somber and moody. The cats avoided him.

Frustrated, he cried because he couldn't master it. We cried with him. The day came for the scout meeting and he still sat in the same spot with a furrowed brow, fussing over the complexity of it all. We fretted over our lack of ability to teach such a simple task and spoke quietly about not taking him to the den meeting that night, to spare him—and ourselves—embarrassment.

I nearly opened my mouth to tell him that it wasn't important for him to learn to tie his shoes, and I fully intended to let him off the hook. But before I did that, his older sister spoke up and suggested a new idea.

"Brian," she softly asked, "why don't you try closing your eyes? Loop your laces over one another and see if you can tie your shoe in your imagination. That way, if you get up to go someplace early, before the sun comes up, you can tie your shoes in the dark."

It worked. Brian sat, with eyes tightly shut, and tied a perfect knot on his right shoe. Without looking up, he crossed laces on his left shoe and tied another perfect knot.

His mother quickly dressed him in his scout uniform, and we all raced to his meeting.

Brian went first. A dozen other scouts and their families sat quietly, almost reverently, and watched in awe as Cub

Scout Brian Lewis May, with eyes closed and tongue out, earned a badge that may well have been the Congressional Medal of Honor and an Olympic Gold Medal rolled into one. Congratulatory hugs commenced and tears of joy fell.

Brian won more than a merit badge that day; he turned something complex and difficult into something ordinary, small, and simple. When he found a new way to solve the problem, it became a significant event, a milestone act of greatness. Brian still ties his shoes with his eyes closed, the way his big sister suggested so many years ago. And he taught his little sister to tie her shoes in the dark just like him.

Since then, I believe that when things get tough and I can't find the solution to a problem, I just close my eyes and find a different way.

A former Disney executive, radio broadcasting owner/manager, fledgling writer, patio tomato farmer, and Intergalactic Caribbean Horseshoe Champion twelve years running, BOB MAY currently lives in Dallas, Texas, in proximity to three grandchildren who are in need of a lot of spoiling.

Life Is Wonderfully Ridiculous

CLAUDE KNOBLER

When I was eighteen, a friend asked if I'd like to deliver singing telegrams in Manhattan while dressed as a gorilla. It wasn't anything I ever expected to do, but I was unemployed and the gorilla mask muffled my lack of singing ability. So I took the job.

Soon after, I heard about another job, this time at the Empire State Building entertaining tourists by posing as King Kong. As one of the few applicants with prior gorilla experience, I was a shoo-in. When the summer ended and it got too cold to be on the observatory deck, even while wearing a gorilla suit, another friend asked if I'd like to be a private detective. I said, "Yes, ever since I was six." After that, I moved to Los Angeles and found myself getting paid to watch movies as a film critic for morning radio shows.

Somewhere between the gorilla suits, the detective job, and eating all that popcorn, I realized something about myself: I believe in the ridiculous.

I was raised in a traditional home where I was taught the value of hard work. I was determined to be determined. But a funny thing happened, or didn't happen. I struggled to become rich and famous, to build a successful career in Hollywood and largely failed; I relaxed, and the ridiculous just came along.

It's not easy trusting in the ridiculous. When my friends ask what my career plans are, I sometimes feel like Linus waiting for the Great Pumpkin to appear. How can I tell them I have no plans—that I'm just waiting for the ridiculous to happen?

Now my main job is something that would have seemed ridiculous when I was in my "determined" phase: I'm a stay-at-home father to three children, and the story of one of them is particularly ridiculous. And wonderful. Ridiculously wonderful.

Five years ago, I read an article about Ethiopian children orphaned by the AIDS epidemic. The idea that my wife and I would adopt a child, when we already had two kids, seemed crazy. The notion that a dying woman in

Africa would gently give me her five-year-old to raise because she could not, seemed horribly absurd. But now my wife and I are the proud parents of Clay, Grace, and Nati, our beautiful twelve-year-old Ethiopian-born son, who enters our kitchen singing at the top of his lungs most every morning.

The ridiculous isn't always funny—Nati's life certainly hasn't been. And the ridiculous can be hard work. As any stay-at-home parent can tell you, some days three children can feel like a hundred.

But when I look at my gorilla-heavy résumé, when I see all three of my kids laughing, when I think about how much less my life would have been if I'd settled for what I thought I'd wanted, I realize I don't much care about the sensible things I once did. It's the ridiculous I love.

And I've got the gorilla suits to prove it.

CLAUDE KNOBLER, of Santa Monica, California, is the author of two novels and "The Boy in the Photo," an unpublished memoir about his family's adoption of his Ethiopian-born son. He also writes his own comic strip, "Capes," which can be seen on Facebook.

Never Give Up

M. C. HACKETT

Never, ever give up.

My father said it to me for the first time nearly thirty years ago. He gripped his sooty hands around the steering wheel of his beat-up Chevy truck and stared out through the windshield, while the wipers batted away big, fluffy, white snowflakes. "You just can't. You can't ever give up. No matter how hard it gets. No matter how it hurts."

He spoke the well-chosen words firmly and tight-lipped, while his head nodded to the rhythm of his speech. I don't remember why he was telling me to never give up, I only remember that he never stopped doing so after that day. Now, I remember these words, whenever I do anything challenging.

My dad was notorious for giving his "I'll tell ya what" speeches to my seven siblings and me after each one of our basketball, baseball, football, and field hockey games—but those lectures would come many years later.

On that particular snowy day I was only five years old and I hadn't even picked up a sport yet. I hadn't yet earned the right to hear one of his go-get-em speeches. I hadn't yet missed a free-throw shot. I hadn't yet stood over the plate and watched the third strike pass without swinging my bat. I hadn't yet only received a 98 on a test. ("Where are the other two points?" he would ask.) To be honest I don't think I ever did anything to warrant the oft-heard never-quit speech in its many variations, but that didn't stop him from giving it.

Like him, and like all his kids, I worked my ass off from the day I was born just to keep up, just to survive. But, still we heard it from him:

"If you give up, someone else will eat the last and only piece of bread. If you give up, you can't win. If you give up, you only have yourself to blame. If you give up, you'll live a life of regrets. Only the strongest, fittest, and ablest survive. Only those who go the distance, finish the race. Only those who work for it, earn it. Perseverance is everything, kid. It's the only thing."

Seventeen years later when he showed up with a U-Haul rigged to his pick-up outside my apartment in Nebraska, I hung my head and couldn't bear to look at him, knowing all the pep talks and lectures he'd given me in that truck. Seeing him standing there, I was sure I had let him down. There I stood, almost nine months' pregnant and the father of my child long gone. I had called my dad twenty-four hours earlier to tell him I had given up. I couldn't do it all alone—raising a kid, living thousands of miles away from home.

We sat in silence for the nearly twenty-hour drive. He didn't say much, but he didn't have to. Without a speech, my father lived the lesson he was trying to teach me for so long. He really didn't ever give up—*even on me.* And because he didn't give up, I didn't either. Somehow I got through those first few lonely nights with an infant, the long work days, the financial struggles, the heartbreak, and the disappointment, because every day I heard my dad's words, over and over, and I too shook my head to the rhythm of the speech as I rocked my newborn daughter, *I will never, ever give up.*

M. C. HACKETT is the mother of Brigid Claire, eleven, and Colm Francis, five. She is now married to Greg Hackett Jr., who adopted Brigid in 2005. Ms. Hackett is a book editor for St. Anthony Messenger Press in Cincinnati, Ohio, a freelance writer, and an adjunct English professor. Her forthcoming novel, *Proof of Heaven*, will be published in 2011.

The Choice to Do It Over Again

DANIEL FLANAGAN

I don't know why I came to the decision to become a loser, but I know I made the choice at a young age. Sometime in the middle of fourth grade, I stopped trying. By the time I was in seventh grade, I was your typical degenerate: lazy, rebellious, disrespectful. I had lost all social graces. I was terminally hip and fatally cool.

It wasn't long after that I dropped out of school and continued my downward spiral. Hard physical labor was the consequence for the choices I made as an adolescent. At the age of twenty-one, I was hopelessly lost, and using drugs as a way to deal with the fact that I was illiterate and stuck in a dead-end job carrying roof shingles up a ladder all day.

But now I believe in do-overs, in the chance to do it all again. And I believe that do-overs can be made at any point in your life, if you have the right motivation. Mine came from a surprising source.

It was September 21, 2002, when my son Blake was born. It's funny that after a life of avoiding responsibility, now I was in charge of something so fragile. Over the years, as I grew into the title of Dad, I began to learn something about myself. In a way, Blake and I were both learning to walk, talk, work, and play for the first time. I began my do-over.

It took me almost three years to learn how to read. I started with my son's books. Over and over, I practiced reading books to him until I remembered all the words in every one of them. I began to wonder if it were possible for me to go back to school. I knew I wanted to be a good role model, so after a year and a half and a lot of hard work, I passed my GED test on my son's fourth birthday. This may not sound like much, and I'm surely not trying to get praise for doing something that should have been done in the first place, but all things considered it was one of the best days in my life. Today, I'm a full-time college student, studying to become a sociologist.

It's funny, growing up I always heard these great turn-around stories of triumph over shortcomings. But I never thought they applied to me. Now I believe it's a choice anyone can make: to do it all over again.

DANIEL FLANAGAN lives in Redford, Michigan, with his wife and son, Blake, and daughter, Gabby. He builds sheds and garages for a living. Mr. Flanagan wrote this essay for an English 101 class at a local community college where he is studying sociology.

The Wonders of the Future

SCOTT SHACKELFORD

I believe in the power of science fiction. Not just for its capacity to transform dreams into reality, but also for its power to bond together those who share a common vision of the future. For me, that's true for my relationship with my dad. Some fathers and sons bond over sports, or fishing, or hunting. My dad and I bond over *Star Trek*. We tried demolition derbies, monster truck rallies, and even a trip to Disney World, but one of my earliest memories wasn't Mickey, but a Klingon battle cruiser menacingly de-cloaking in the *Enterprise* viewscreen.

Over the years, nearly every setting and situation has become a galaxy far, far away for my dad and me. When it's snowing at night, we're not driving along some dark street in Indiana, but going at warp speed with stars whipping by. Both of us are thinking it, without needing to say a word. When we're rummaging around in the car looking for a map, we quote Khan from *Star Trek II*: "The override, where's the override?" We can't say "two weeks" without sounding like Arnold Schwarzenegger in *Total Recall* when he's going through customs on Mars. A new foreign language phrase that neither of us has heard becomes "klaatu barada nikto" from *The Day the Earth Stood Still*.

When either of us Googles something and sends it to the other, we invariably preface it by writing, "From an entry in the Encyclopedia Galactica," quoting Isaac Asimov's *Foundation* series. Nightmares become "monsters from the id," vis-à-vis *Forbidden Planet*. Even my choice of expletives has been affected: I now use "frak" from *Battlestar Galactica* rather than the colloquial alternative. The summation of these visions of other universes has together created a private universe for my dad and me.

Gene Rodenberry, creator of *Star Trek*, once said, "Science fiction is a way of thinking, a way of logic that bypasses a lot of nonsense. It allows people to look directly at important subjects."

A lifetime of sci-fi has influenced more than just my relationship with my dad, but has also helped me shape my own hopes for the future. I'm now a freelance science writer, I am hooked on *Nova*, and I grab the *Science Times* even before the comics. My doctoral dissertation is on property rights in the commons, including outer space, and I spent my first summer of law school working at the NASA general counsel's office.

Yes, sci-fi has made me into a nerd, but it also has been a source of joy for my family, and has made me an optimist while enabling me to think critically about the perils of technology. Thank you to those authors who have shared their visions; the world—and my family—are better for it.

And thank you to my dad, who is both the best storyteller and the best man I have ever known because he helped realize the truth of Tennyson's words, "For I dipped into the future, far as human eyes could see, saw the vision of the world, and all the wonders that would be."

A native of Indianapolis, SCOTT SHACKELFORD studied economics and political science at Indiana University, international relations at Cambridge, and law at Stanford. He is currently an assistant professor at Indiana University where he enjoys writing about law and technology, traveling, and continuing to share a love of science fiction with his father.

The Best Legacy I Can Leave

DOUG ANDREWS

I believe in keeping garage doors open.

When I was a teenager, my father told me one of his lifelong goals was to live past sixty—the age at which his father, a minister, had closed the doors to his garage, started his car, and ended his life from breathing in the carbon monoxide. That was in 1941.

In 1976, my father achieved his goal of living longer than his dad by marking his sixty-first birthday. There wasn't much of a celebration, though: my parents' marriage was disintegrating, and my father was losing his battle with alcohol. A year later, he killed himself as his father had: sitting in a car behind a closed garage door, the motor running.

I remember when I got news of his death. I sprinted across my college quad in bare feet on a November night, running until I thought my chest would burst. After the funeral, I went back to school and got on with things. For years thereafter, my life did not appear disrupted by my father's suicide, at least not outwardly. Inwardly, it was a different story. After repeated bouts of depression, I began worrying that my paternal DNA had already predetermined my fate: that if the going got too rough for me someday, I also might turn to suicide.

Perhaps in anticipation of that day, I unconsciously began my own version of closing garage doors. From my midtwenties through my early forties, I lived alone in a small tenement apartment, working a succession of low-level jobs despite having an Ivy League education. I frittered away relationships and money, periodically isolating myself from friends and family, and doing my share of binge drinking.

While I never actually felt suicidal, I came to see that I was committing a kind of living suicide—not one in which a life was taken, but one in which life was no longer embraced. This realization came to me after spending years in therapy, going on antidepressant drugs, and experiencing the death of my mother. Once I understood what was happening, I slowly started to open the doors I had closed earlier on my life. In my early forties, I met Barbara and we soon married; we had two beautiful sons in short order and another is on the way. We bought a house and found community in our new hometown. We've even agreed to teach a Sunday school class this winter.

I can empathize with my father and grandfather, not to mention the thirty thousand other Americans who take their lives each year. But for the sake of my sons, the family history of suicide I inherited stops with me. To live a long, full life and die from natural causes may turn out to be the best possible legacy I can leave them. I resolve that the garage doors my father and grandfather chose to close on their lives will stay open wide in my lifetime and, I hope, in the lives of my sons.

DOUG ANDREWS works as a technical writer in New York, and lives with his wife and three sons in Glen Ridge, New Jersey.

To Be the Best Humans
We Can Be

TIM WILSON

I believe that my actions define my beliefs, not my words.

I wrote a letter to my kids a few years ago. It's three pages long, and it sums up what I've learned in four decades of life. My kids are too young to understand now, but by the time they reach adulthood, they will have heard most of the advice in that letter: live in the moment, do not attach yourself to physical things, treat others the way you would like to be treated, find happiness in the service of others, make the most out of today, follow your dreams, don't take yourself too seriously, be aware that there are hypocrites and manipulators in the world, et cetera.

I sealed the letter in a plain white envelope, and wrote instructions not to open it unless something horrible happened to me. A "Marvin the Martian" magnet holds it to the side of my musty gray metal locker at work. It is surrounded by police uniforms, spare change, "tribute of mourning" ribbons for my badge (to honor fallen colleagues), pictures of my kids, *The Far Side* cartoons, poems, scraps of paper with handwritten notes, business cards, dust, and lint—remnants of almost twenty years of serving others.

As a police officer, I've seen life snuffed out or irrevocably changed in an instant. I realize that could happen to me at any time. Yet knowing that letter is there in my locker makes me more comfortable with my own mortality. If something does happen to me, my children will get that letter. In it, they will read about my love for them and about the advice that I want to pass on to them when they are old enough to understand it.

Every day, when I open my locker, I see the letter. It reminds me to be careful at work, and to show my children and the people I come into contact with that I truly understand and practice everything I've written. If that day comes and my children finally read the letter, I hope that because of my actions, they will take my written beliefs to heart and improve upon my example.

But for me, it's not enough to write down my beliefs. I try to be the best person I can be every day—even in very difficult circumstances, even with offensive people. I'm more successful some days than others. I curse too much, sometimes I'm cynical, and I don't go to church as often as I should. I also get depressed, yell at my kids occasionally, and sometimes I'm not as loving or as compassionate as I should be. In fact, I am far from perfect, but I hope my children will eventually realize that perfection is an illusion. What really matters is that, instead of just writing about our beliefs, we all take action to be the best humans we can be.

SERGEANT TIM WILSON has been a member of the California Highway Patrol for twenty-three years. He is currently assigned to the Mariposa CHP office, near Yosemite National Park. Sergeant Wilson enjoys photography and spending time with his wife and three children.

Work Is a Blessing

LIEUTENANT GENERAL RUSSEL HONORÉ

I grew up in Lakeland, Louisiana, one of twelve children. We all lived on my parents' subsistence farm. We grew cotton, sugar cane, corn, hogs, and chickens, and we had a large garden, but it didn't bring in much cash. So when I was twelve, I got a part-time job on a dairy farm down the road, helping to milk cows. We milked sixty-five cows at five o'clock in the morning and again at two in afternoon, seven days a week.

In the kitchen one Saturday before daylight, I remember complaining to my father and grandfather about having to go milk those cows. My father said, "Ya know, boy, to work is a blessing."

I looked at those two men who'd worked harder than I ever had—my father eking out a living on that farm, and my grandfather, farming and working as a carpenter during the Depression. I had a feeling I had been told something really important, but it took many years before it had sunk in.

Going to college was a rare privilege for a kid from Lakeland, Louisiana. My father told me if I picked something to study that I liked doing, I'd always look forward to my work. But he also added, "Even having a job you hate is better than not having a job at all." I wanted to be a farmer, but I joined the ROTC program to help pay for college. And what started out as an obligation to the Army became a way of life that I stayed committed to for thirty-seven years, three months, and three days.

In the late 1980s, during a visit to Bangladesh, I saw a woman with a baby on her back, breaking bricks with a hammer. I asked a Bangladesh military escort why they weren't using a machine, which would have been a lot easier. He told me a machine would put that lady out of work. Breaking those bricks meant she'd earn enough money to feed herself and her baby that day. And as bad as that woman's job was, it was enough to keep a small family alive. It reminded me of my father's words: to work is a blessing.

Serving in the United States Army overseas, I saw a lot of people like that woman in Bangladesh. And I have come to believe that people without jobs are not free. They are victims of crime, the ideology of terrorism, poor health, depression, and social unrest. These victims become the illegal immigrants, the slaves of human trafficking, the drug dealers, the street gang members. I've seen it over and over again on the U.S. border, in Somalia, the Congo, Afghanistan, and in New Orleans. People who have jobs can have a home, send their kids to school, develop a sense of pride, contribute to the good of the community, and even help others. When we can work, we're free. We're blessed.

I don't think I'll ever quit working. I'm retired from the Army, but I'm still working to help people be prepared for disaster. And I may get to do a little farming someday, too. I'm not going to stop. I believe in my father's words. I believe in the blessing of work.

RETIRED LIEUTENANT GENERAL RUSSEL HONORÉ led federal recovery efforts following Hurricanes Katrina and Rita in 2005. He also held command positions in the United States, Korea, and Germany, and he supported Department of Defense planning for numerous natural disasters.

Hands at Rest

⁓

JOHN R. CORRIGAN

When I think of my father, I remember his hands. Liver-spotted and dexterous, hands that tied flies and built wooden toys for children at Christmas. Those hands that palmed my chest and stomach when I learned to swim now cannot break free of the bedrails—or of the esophageal cancer that slowly strangles him.

It is late March 2006, and the nurse has tied my father's hands to steel bedrails so that in his morphine-induced state he won't pull out his IV. Needle pricks from three weeks in the hospital have left the backs of his hands bruised and yellowed. I look at his hands and remember how strong they used to be, how so many things I know how to do came from watching his hands.

My father was a teacher. Not by trade but by nature. He understood the catch-phrase "teachable moment" better than most educators.

I am five or six, freezing in an ice shack on the Kennebec River, smelts sizzling in a frying pan close by. His hands busy tying flies, he says, "You should help one person each day."

Years later, in the front yard, with a rake in his hand, he tells me "Marry your best friend, son. That's what I did."

The lectures didn't end when I grew up, either. I even looked forward to his monthly phone calls, sure to find a lesson somewhere. He would make sure I was replacing the windows the right way, or make sure I was not turning into "one of those awful Little League parents." I would groan, "Dad, I'm thirty-five." "And you still need a lecture," he'd say. "Sad, isn't it?"

His most important lesson didn't come as a lecture. My sister and I stand in the hallway awaiting Dad's return from the x-ray lab. They have taken him off the ventilator to see if the mechanical breathing apparatus allowed his lungs to rest and heal to where he can breathe on his own. We are praying for a miracle. At the sound of a bed coming toward us, wheels grinding dully, we look up. Dad raises his hand, and the nurse stops pushing the bed.

My chest gets tighter when I look down at him. He is bald, his eyes sunken. A month earlier, my daughters, ages eight and five, did not immediately recognize him.

"How are you doing?" As stupid as that question is, I can think of nothing else.

"It could be worse," he says.

"It could be worse?" I repeat. "Dad, how the hell could this get any worse?"

"There was a little girl from the children's cancer floor coming out of x-ray when I went in," he says simply. "Looked like my granddaughter. That would be worse."

We will sit with Dad during his final night, the distance between him and me widening like gaps between his final sandpaper breaths. At 7 A.M. the nurse will say the obvious, and I will look toward the ceiling as if watching Dad drive away after visiting his grandchildren. Only this time there will be no wave, just a disjointed feeling of permanence.

I believe dignity may be the most challenging attribute a parent can pass on to a child—dying with it, even more so. When the nurse wheels the bed away, Dad's hands are no longer tied down. Now they are folded peacefully across his chest.

JOHN R. CORRIGAN is a former journalist and current member of the English faculty at Pomfret School in Connecticut. A former columnist for *Golf Today Magazine*, he now writes a weekly blog for "Type M for Murder," and his articles have appeared in *Writer's Journal*, *Nova*, and *Dutchess Magazine*. Mr. Corrigan has published five novels, each of which took between six and twelve months to write. This essay took him eighteen months.

The Myths of Manhood

ANDREW RIUTTA

I grew up in the Upper Peninsula of Michigan, a region known for its harsh winters and profound isolation. Many of my relatives immigrated there from Finland and Sweden in the latter part of the nineteenth century—in search of a better life, I suppose. Most of the men worked as farmers, miners, or lumberjacks, while the women stayed home to cook and sew. And pray.

My grandfather could be quite jovial at times. On first impression, you'd never know that he was an uncompromising and often brutal sort. My father was much the same, and so—naturally—it was instilled within me that a man is only worth his brawn: work for ten hours or more a day, don't complain, but then settle the score late at night with a twelve pack and foul mouth. For years I walked around with this chip on my shoulder, believing grit alone could suffice as a disposition for living. And just like my kin, I stumbled in and out of the types of jobs that left me with rough and callused hands—thus authenticating myself as a loyal son. A true man.

In the summer of 2000, my girlfriend informed me that she was pregnant—that *we* were pregnant. Recognizing that this was a situation I would not be able to muscle my way through, I immediately felt the blood leave my face. It seemed I was standing on unfamiliar ground. At that moment, I told myself I could never be a good father, and so it would probably be best if I didn't even try. I explained my feelings to my girlfriend, but she simply said she'd have the baby with or without me. There was so much courage in her eyes that I quickly realized it was something I'd never really had. So I decided to give it a chance. To give myself a chance.

Next month, our daughter will be ten years old, and although my hands are still very much callused from the many abrasive things they've held over the years, my daughter has taught me that these hands are more than capable of the softest touch—and only within this capacity do they reveal their actual strength.

I believe most every man has stood toe to toe with himself in the bathroom mirror, shadow boxing in an attempt to maintain those many myths that say he must be unbreakable and unafraid. But I also believe every man owes it to himself, as well as those he loves, to turn away from that mirror, and instead gather his strength from a willingness to be as gentle as he can possibly be in this increasingly hostile world.

ANDREW RIUTTA lives in northern Michigan with his ten-year-old daughter, Issabella. He is a recent recipient of the William J. Shaw memorial prize for poetry, and in the spring of 2009, he began working on a book to be titled *Something Shaped like a Rocket*.

Love with No Limits

SCOTT ZUCKER

I was twenty-one when my parents asked me their question, "What provisions have you made for having children?" I had not long before told them that I was gay and it was important for them to know. Frankly, I had so thoroughly convinced myself of the incongruity of parenthood and gay life that I had given up on the idea of ever becoming a father. My response was naive, even for me: "You mean I can?"

Fast-forward twenty years and I found myself with a loving partner and the money from the sale of our house to hire a surrogate to have a child for us. Our son Aiden was born in August 2002, followed in April 2005 by twin boys, Bram and Cade. In many ways my life had finally begun.

For a while, years before I had kids, I would volunteer my time speaking to college classes about what it was like to be gay. In most of these classes the question of whether I wanted children would almost always come up. One day a student stood and spoke ominously of the harm he felt a child would suffer growing up in such a family—how any child doomed to be raised by two dads or two moms would suffer deep psychological wounds. I countered with studies I'd read documenting no long-term psychological harm from being a child of a gay parent and, in my opinion, having experienced life as a gay child, I had learned that it is the adversity we experience that better prepares us to handle life. I don't know if I convinced him of anything, but his words left me feeling isolated.

Because of encounters like this I've always tended to view the world in partisan terms—us against them; Republican versus Democrat, gay versus straight. I know I'm not alone in this. But now as a new parent, when I'm at the pool acting as both lifeguard and flotation device, I know I share a multitude of life experiences, not the least of which is the practice of giving love with no limits, a joy that gives perspective on a life often lived in remote control. And what's more, I see my mother and father in my own parenting and understand at long last, how wholly we are alike.

I believe in the transformational power of parenthood.

Becoming a parent has united me with a family much larger than my own—a world of moms and dads passionately and selflessly caring for their kids. Every day I see someone or something that makes me realize how being a parent has transformed my world, allowing me to feel as if I've returned home, apart from a self-segregation I didn't even know existed.

In between time-outs and helping the kids with their homework, SCOTT ZUCKER runs a successful landscape architectural firm in Southern California. He and David, his soul mate and partner of thirteen years, were legally married in 2008.

An Ordinary Adventure

∽

DAVID LINTVEDT

When I was a boy, I dreamed of the adventures I would have when I grew up. I wanted to be a cop, so I made up stories of fighting crime, saving people's lives, and making a difference in the world. When I was in high school and college, I wanted to become a newspaper reporter. I imagined myself sending in stories from some conflict in Central America or the Middle East, telling the truth about what was happening in parts of the world where the truth is not always clear. At other times in my life, I have simply thought of just hitting the road, moving from place to place and taking each new day and each new place as an adventure, then writing about it.

My life did not turn out as I had imagined it. Instead of living a life of adventure, my life is very ordinary. I work at an office job, with an hour commute each way. I own an old house that demands a lot of attention. I pay most of my bills on time, go to church, and make sure there's food in the refrigerator.

My life is good, but sometimes I feel a little sorry for myself for having traded a life of excitement for a life of quiet responsibility, holding down a job and raising my daughter. But, when I think about it, I realize that *this* is the adventure! What could be more challenging, more exciting than being a father? In my childhood dreams of adventure, I never imagined myself as a single parent, and I had no way of knowing how much of an adventure it would be.

Of course, I never planned on being a single father. When Hannah was born I thought I would be raising her with her mother, as a family. However, things did not turn out the way I thought they would, as our marriage faltered and then failed before my daughter had her third birthday. When it was clear that the marriage was over and we had to separate, I did not think twice about taking Hannah with me when I moved out to my own place.

I have found adventure in changing diapers, waking up to calm my daughter after a nightmare, and chasing loose hamsters in her room. There was adventure in the many trips to the doctor for earaches and runny noses, in vacation trips to the Badlands, and imaginary expeditions to hunt for bears or aliens. I also find adventure in going over homework assignments that confuse me almost as much as learning about the complicated social lives of teenage girls!

I believe that adventure is where you find it.

The adventure of being a single parent has been amazing, overwhelming, frustrating, and incredibly difficult, yet I can see no better way to have spent these years of my life. This experience has formed a strong bond between my daughter and me—a bond that may not have been created if life had taken a different turn. I am glad that I have had the opportunity to be a father, and I would not trade this experience for any of my boyhood dreams of adventure. This adventure is far more rewarding.

DAVID LINTVEDT was born in the Bronx, New York, then was adopted by a college professor and his wife who raised him in East Orange, New Jersey. He has a bachelor's degree in English from Upsala College and a master of divinity from the Lutheran Theological Seminary of Philadelphia. Mr. Lintvedt enjoys writing, reading, cycling, and volunteering at his church. He lives with his daughter, Hannah, along with two dogs and three cats in East Greenville, Pennsylvania.

My Earthly Father

MARGO FRAZIER

Because my earthly father was always accessible, I always think of my heavenly father in the same context. Daddy was someone I feared, respected, admired, and called on in times of need, and that is how I view God.

Daddy was just. Whenever I was in trouble, he would lecture me for half an hour before he got to the spanking. Sometimes, the lecture was all I'd get. He always gave me a chance to explain. I believe God gives me the same opportunity.

Daddy had dreams, disappointments, and fall outs with in-laws. He worried about bills, tuition, and medical expenses. But he persevered through it all, demonstrating strength of will and courage. He never complained, whined, or begged for anything. He did cry from time to time, usually over something he wished for his children. God has a softer side too, the "mother heart of God."

Daddy loved Country and Western music, and he would do his best to play the guitar while Mama sang. Sometimes he would recruit me to sing along. That is how I honored him; this is how I worship today.

Daddy went to war, killed a man, and had nightmares about it. But when I joined the military, he was proud that I wanted to be a protector of my country. I believe God wants us to defend what we believe in.

When I was a teenager, Daddy became my nemesis. At the same time I became rebellious against God. I didn't want to abide by the rules and, even though I fought my dad, he would not budge from his stance. But I always knew exactly where he stood. I know where God stands, too.

Daddy worked for forty years to feed ten hungry mouths, and he made sure we all had shoes. I believe that God also provides for my daily needs.

Daddy took pride in his appearance, but when he wanted to get some sun, he would put on a skimpy pair of swimming trunks and get out there and cut the grass. I believe God wants us to relax sometimes and enjoy nature.

Daddy never worried about himself, but always took the time to kiss my mother, and every once in a while he would take her out to dinner. I believe that God cares more about us than we do about Him.

Daddy smoked, drank beer, cursed worse than any sailor, and had a very eloquent way of taking the Lord's name in vain. He couldn't be perfect, for he was not God.

Though he wasn't perfect, I believe everyone could use a daddy like mine. He is the best example of what an earthly father should be.

MARGO FRAZIER grew up in Memphis, Tennessee, and later joined the Navy, where she served as a photographer's mate. Encouraged by an English professor to pursue writing as a creative outlet, Ms. Frazier has had several pieces published recently. She currently lives with her two daughters and one granddaughter in Jacksonville, Florida.

The Give-and-Take of Grief

∽

MICHAEL NEWLAND

I believe that grieving is good for you. As a culture, I feel we've forgotten how to grieve, and last year, I had the opportunity to remember.

My wife was seven months pregnant when her blood pressure spiked. Her liver started to shut down, so the doctors performed a Cesarean and our son was delivered to save both of their lives.

The first time I saw my son, he was in an incubator with nurses clearing his airways. He looked at me, like a dolphin surfacing to look at a fisherman, and then resubmerged when the team took him away to stabilize him. He was the smallest, most fragile baby I'd ever seen.

Over the next two weeks, my wife's health stabilized; my son's condition, however, deteriorated. The lungs of premature babies are as delicate and tenuous as a spider web, and they shred at the slightest pressure. I wanted to put him inside my chest and give him my lungs to breathe with. We went from holding him, to putting a hand on his head, to, at the end, with all the tubes and wires, only being able to lay one finger on the back of his hand. His lungs failed, and we had to let him go.

We never heard him cry. My wife and I, first-time parents, held him as he died, and we bathed him, washed his hair, and dressed him before he was cremated. In my mind, I could see an angel close her hand around my son like he was a gold coin and slip him into her pocket.

As each day passes, you close your eyes and let your grief slide through your fingers, one rough, cold link after another, until your loss settles deep inside you. It is a give-and-take between you and your grief, a tension that rolls your emotions back and forth. And at first you are certain that your life is going to capsize and you will drown. Eventually, the grief will ground you and give you stability in troubled times.

I am a better husband, a better father, and a better man for my loss—I'm kinder, more empathetic, and have different priorities. Our marriage was re-forged, the impurities burned out of the relationship by the furnace of our son's death. To be with your child nearly every minute of his life is a gift few parents get, and my son died in the arms of people who loved him.

Ten months ago, my wife gave birth to our healthy daughter, and I am filled with a joy made greater by the loss of my son, because I know now what we have. The angel has extended her open hand to me. When my daughter turned to look at me for the first time, I picked her up and held her with everything I had.

MICHAEL NEWLAND is a staff archaeologist with the Anthropological Studies Center at Sonoma State University. He lives with his daughter, Caitie Belle, in Santa Rosa, California. Mr. Newland wrote his essay as part of a hospice grief group.

The Lawn Is Life

GREG VESSAR

I believe that mowing the lawn is my life. Maybe I'd better explain. "Taking care of the lawn," my father always said, "is like taking care of your life. Finishing a job well done soothes the soul."

As I was crouched low putting gas in a tank that was over half full, he elaborated, as if I'd asked him to. I was fourteen and didn't ask, but that never slowed down Dad.

"First, never start anything without being prepared. You gotta have a full tank of gas. Even if gas is in the mower, top it off so you can finish without stopping." Never one to waste a soapbox, he related mowing to life every chance he got. "Maintain the mower so it runs like a charm." Without breaking stride, he spit his tobacco juice into a well-positioned beer can whose top had been removed with sharp tin snips. "A clean mower will run with little to slow 'er down."

"Don't mow crooked," Dad always said. "Mow straight and be efficient. Mow with a purpose, no need to be fancy and try to be something you're not." I guess, in his own way, my dad was quoting Shakespeare's *Hamlet*, "To thine own self be true." I got it when Polonius said it, but it took me a while to get that my dad was saying the exact same thing.

Although it took me some time to relate this to my life, my dad's philosophy finally makes sense. Maintaining healthy relationships with the people around us is like mowing the lawn. I have remained happily married and in love with the same woman for more than twenty years. We keep the blades clean by being open and honest, and by topping off each other's tank. It takes patience and time, but I believe in keeping that particular mower clean and running well.

My dad also constantly lectured my little brother and me about cleaning our fingernails every time we went someplace. I guess it was like keeping the edges of the lawn neat and trimmed. "Don't forget to trim the edges of the yard. I don't want people to think I neglect what's mine," he would yell as he spit tobacco. Whenever we headed to the truck to go into town, he would ask to see our fingernails. "Hold on there, let me see those fingernails. They better be clean." My brother and I always had dirty fingernails. We grew up on a farm and lived outside. If our nails didn't pass his inspection, he reached in his pocket and retrieved his little Buck pocketknife, handed it to me, and said, "Clean those fingernails. First impressions is everything," as he spit another bull's-eye of tobacco juice.

Now, as an adult, I finally understand. I believe that first impressions are a portrait of who we are and what we can accomplish when we care for the things given to us. I believe in taking care of the things in my life that are important to me.

So, my fingernails are clean. I think I'll go mow my lawn.

GREG VESSAR was born and raised in a small town in the Midwest. He and his wife, Melissa, have been married for twenty-one years. Mr. Vessar currently teaches language arts at a public school in California.

The Bricks in the Wall
Around My Heart

JUDD PILLOT

Can I call my essay, "This I Really Want to Believe"? Because when friends tell me, "Of course your son wants nothing to do with you now. He's seventeen, but he'll come back," I really want to believe them. I really want to believe that when my son, Jacob, calls me a "weenus," or tells me I need to take a "chill pill," that underneath he loves me and he's just slapping the old lion with a teenage paw.

When Jacob does "come back," I hope it'll make up for all the angst and anger we've been going through. Jacob is the older of my two sons. Outwardly, he is cocky, cool, and by far the more rebellious. But I'm certain his bravado is born of insecurity. Fear masquerading as swagger. Hard shell. Soft, sweet center.

"Daddy, you take down the bricks
from the wall around my heart."

Jacob was five when he wrote that Father's Day card. He drew a cartoon heart peeking through a hole in a brick wall. I haven't gotten a message like that in a long time. Instead it seems each year we added a few more bricks to the wall. At thirteen, he proposed:

"Dad, why don't we just fight
for control of the house now?"

"First of all, you'll have to fight your mother," I replied with a laugh. Inside I was hoping he'd heard that line in a movie, or a TV show—that it wasn't an original idea. Then at fifteen, when he said:

"I don't do what's right because you tell me,
I do what's right because I tell myself what's right."

I really wanted to believe in how wise a statement that was—how self-possessed and aware a kid would have to be to even come up with that declaration. Inside I was wondering if it was just more push-back.

Being driven and focused, I've always urged both boys to challenge themselves in every endeavor. I encouraged them to have goals and to take the steps to achieve them. But over the years, the more I challenged Jacob, the more he resisted.

In hindsight, I focused too much on wanting him to do things my way. And all that "focus" made me blind to the fact that he might have had his own way. I no longer see the Jacob I want him to be, or who I think he should be. I now see Jacob: a remarkable young man with or without my guidance. He just is.

I have this fantasy where Jacob and I sit around having a beer, reminiscing. He says, "Gee, Dad, I really put you through hell." I say, "Well, I could've lightened up a bit." He chuckles, "I actually called you a weenus?" Then we laugh. I hug him tight, and he hugs me right back, just as tight. And right then I know my friends were telling the truth.

This I most definitely do believe: Whether or not I am, or have ever been a "weenus," I do need the occasional "chill pill." Because someday soon my remarkable son will be out on his own. Control of the house will revert back to me (fingers crossed), and I'm going to miss him like hell.

JUDD PILLOT has written and produced television comedy for over twenty-five years, and he has recently branched into drama and feature films. He's also taught creative writing and TV production. Mr. Pillot lives in Los Angeles with his wife, Karen, and has two sons, Nick, eighteen, and Jacob, now twenty-one. They are getting closer.

The First Breath

KAZ SUSSMAN

I am a stone-cold atheist. Yet I find that I believe in miracles, and in my case the miracle is breath—first breath—the first breath of our daughter, who entered this world blue and worn from the long journey of her birth. I was there.

I held her mom's hand, witness to the focus and exhaustion that difficult childbirth can bring, witness to the emerging of life from life. I was there.

It was a hard, slow delivery and our daughter was born low on oxygen. There were none of the expected baby sounds. The doctor and midwife spirited her into an incubator and sucked the mucus from her airways. I was there.

It was scary. Folks can tell you about their child's delivery all day long, and you still won't get it. But be there once and you get it all. It's all about that first breath. And however they managed it, combining science and care, our daughter got the oxygen that she needed.

Through this miracle of breath, the gift of my daughter appeared—a gift I never anticipated having in my life, a sacred trust, a connection so profound that it brought me to tears. There must be a word for that blissed-out epiphany of tears that comes from a heart breaking open as mine did that day.

I was there at her first breath. I looked in her eyes, and my life was transformed. Somehow, from that moment on, I've found that I believe not only in my child but in your child as well.

Perhaps you've seen me around town. I'm the old guy silently blessing young fathers caring for their children. Watching these fathers' faces as their children call to them, "Daddy, look what I've done."

I say to them, "Isn't 'daddy' the best sound you ever heard?"

"You bet," they always say, "the best."

My daughter is now thirty-four, with children of her own. Her partner was there for the births. Life from life, it's an amazing thing, but you have to be there to truly comprehend that moment.

So, what do I believe? I believe in being there for the first breath, and I believe in all of our children. I forever thank my daughter for her part in teaching me this simple truth because, truly, I believe in her.

KAZ SUSSMAN is a carpenter living in a home he built in the Oregon woods from abandoned poems. He does postdisaster inspections for FEMA and has knelt before children who once spoke.

Finding My Father in
a Small World

KATE DEBIEC

When I was younger, before my parents' divorce, there was one phrase I heard so often that even now, nearing the first anniversary of my dad's death, I can hear his voice say . . . with an astounded chuckle and a slow shake of his head, "What a small world!"

He was so predictable with this remark that my brothers and sister and I could be caught miming it behind him almost as soon as he struck up a conversation. It seemed like he could find a connection with anyone: our widowed German land-lady, the Japanese grandmother who watched us a few days a week, the guy in line for the bathroom next to him.

For my father, the world was his Kevin Bacon game. No one was more than two degrees of separation away from being friend or family. No one was a foreigner and the world was always wondrously small.

It wasn't until recently, as I was struggling to find what legacy he'd left me—this man who I hadn't lived with since I was eleven—that I could hear my voice echo his.

Maybe it's inquisitive or maybe it's just plain nosy, but it's something I inherited from him. I think there are a lot of us "small-worlders" out there. The "Oh, really, you grew up in Poughkeepsie, I lived there once," or the "That's such an unusual last name, what's your background?" or the "Did you say you went to Northwestern?" type of person. The person who improbably believes that the woman he or she is speaking with might just know their friend who lives in Nicaragua.

We are those people, who early and often probe for the details that bring us closer to another, looking for some kind of shared history and continue that search wherever we happen to be calling home.

It's possible that this characteristic is born out of necessity or desire to assimilate into new environments. My father had led a wandering childhood. A product of his upbringing, he continued to move every two to three years until his death. We accompanied him around the globe until my parents decided their nomadic life wasn't working, so my siblings and I settled in one spot with my mother. But in our journeys together, my dad showed me how not to be intimidated by boundaries, borders, or new languages and to make companions of strangers whether we were sitting at a bus stop, climbing mountains, or crossing oceans.

I now think those conversations that began with a "Do you know . . . ?" or a "Have you been to . . . ?" were his way of entwining his roots with others, so as to give more strength to his own. Like him, I believe we all share a desire to connect with one another, to discover that we are more alike than at first glance and to find the familiar in this small world.

KATE DEBIEC lives in Seattle, Washington, with her wonderful husband, Josh Veatch. She is an OB-GYN and enjoys crafting, baking, and hiking. Although J.R.R. Tolkien said, "Not all those who wander are lost," Ms. Debiec believes that some who wander may indeed be lost, but she admires those who, like her father when he was alive, continue to search and embrace the journey.

I Am Capable of More
Than I Think I Am

GREGG ROGERS

It is Trisomy 21. It is Down syndrome."

Beyond those words I heard nothing, sitting in the obstetrician's office. The doctor was talking about my unborn daughter, and the results of an amniocentesis. I know there were words after that statement, but I don't remember them. I do remember returning home with my wife and crying on the sofa. I distinctly remember saying, "I don't want this." I didn't want this situation. I didn't want this responsibility. I didn't want to become one of those parents—the parents of a child with a disability.

People told me, "If anyone can handle it, you can."

"Easy for you to say," I thought.

"God never gives you more than you can handle," they reassured me.

"Really? Then why do people have nervous breakdowns?"

"We'll help however we can," they said.

"Fine," I thought. "You have the kid with the developmental delay, and I'll help you out."

For months I was terrified. My wife, Lucy, and I now refer to the period of time leading up to my daughter's birth as "The Pit." We barely spoke to each other because we didn't know what to say. We simply suffered through each day, together, but feeling terribly alone. And then Genevieve was born.

She spent her first eight days in the neonatal intensive care unit at a regional medical center. On each of those eight days I made the 150-mile round trip to see her, because she was my daughter. I sat in a surgical gown in intensive care, holding her in a tangle of tubes and wires, singing the same songs I had sung to other daughters.

On the ninth day, she came home, and I began to realize that my feelings of fear and anxiety had changed in a way that no prenatal screening could ever have predicted.

I now believe Genevieve is here for everyone. I believe Genevieve is taking over the world, one heart at a time— beginning with mine. I believe that what was once our perceived damnation has now become our unexpected salvation.

Genevieve recently turned three and is doing very well for herself. She runs and climbs on everything and loves to wrestle with her two older sisters and her younger brother. She doesn't have a lot of spoken words yet, although her first full sentence turned out to be, "What's up with that?" She does have over 100 signs that allow her to ask for strawberries, pizza, or ice cream, or tell us when she wants to sleep or play on her computer. She goes to a regular preschool three days a week and seems to know more people around town than I do. I laugh every day because of Genevieve.

On my right wrist, I wear a simple silver chain with three little beads on it. I used to say the three beads signified the third chromosome that results in Trisomy 21, Down syndrome. Now when I look at those beads, they simply remind me that I don't ever know as much as I think I do, but I'm always capable of more than I think I am.

GREGG ROGERS is a senior lecturer in the English department at Pennsylvania State University. He spent ten years as a writer, reporter, and editor in New York and Los Angeles. Mr. Rogers and his wife helped found a support group and host a Web site for other families with individuals with Down syndrome in their area.

Teacher

~~

NICK CAPO

In my mother's house, a cedar chest sits in a bedroom corner. Six years ago, after my father died, my mother and I sorted its contents.

Inside, a fifty-year-old black notebook recorded my father's basketball statistics and observations. Junior year of high school: Twenty-two points against Nativity; twenty-seven points against St. Francis. Forty-one points against Regina Coeli; the entire opposing team only scored forty-eight. His senior year: a seventeen-and-one team record; section champs. "High-points man," again and again, but alternating with a teammate. They must have pushed each other.

Growing up, I knew my father was good at basketball. We spent many evenings after he came home from work on outdoor courts across the Pittsburgh area, shooting in fading sunlight, talking over the crickets, until night hid the ball from our eyes. After coaching me, he eventually would announce—apologetically—that it was time to work on a new shot or, usually, on his "jumper." His jump shot was beautiful.

Those who play sports will understand: each sport has its techniques and its beauty. Watching the fluid execution of my father's setup and release and the ball's parabolic arc, hearing the ripping snap of a nothing-but-net basket was awesome.

Until I saw his meticulous notebook, though, I didn't fully understand the intensity with which he studied the game or the depth of his passion for it.

Despite my father's patient efforts, basketball never captured my imagination. Volleyball and reading did, however, and I have records of my own accomplishments. Some are statistics; some, photographs. My parents took one photo when I fell asleep after an exhausting tournament on—in—a plate of spaghetti. Another is a memory of my dad shaking me from a book and saying, "Dinnertime." When I said, "Already?" he laughed so hard and long that tears rolled down his cheeks. I had been reading for eight hours.

This is how it's done, I must have realized, while watching my dad nail thousands of jump shots. If you want to play well, if you want to excel at something, you put in the time. You sweat and struggle when most other people aren't. You practice.

Now, as a college English professor, I know more about how people succeed: they form good habits. During the semester, I take students to computer labs and let them write for one hour. Most days I witness the shift from distraction to concentration as joy captures their minds. "Okay, now count your words," I say. "That's your day's work." I praise specific accomplishments—the ones in which they invested many hours or risked public exposure. "Well done," I told the junior surprised by winning the local library's fiction contest. "Your hard work paid off."

Pride in achievement. Joy in effort. Work as play. My father never attended college, but he knew these truths. He learned them on the basketball court, and he taught them to me.

So I believe in teaching and learning. I believe in practice and hard work. And, finally, I believe in the determined pursuit of excellence.

NICK CAPO is an associate professor of English at Illinois College. He grew up in Pennsylvania, earning a BA and an MFA in English at Pennsylvania State University. Mr. Capo now lives with his wife, Beth, in Jacksonville, Illinois.

Five Dollars of Forgiveness

DANIEL PLASMAN

I believe in the five dollars my father gave me after I burned down the family garage. Though the flames didn't destroy the entire wooden structure, they charred a good portion of it, enough to warrant the arrival of two fire trucks and an impressive gathering of neighbors.

At twelve years of age, I was an arsonist, howbeit an unintentional one. Warm charcoals left from a Sunday evening barbeque found their way into the large cardboard box we used as our garbage receptacle. They got there because, well, I was assigned clean-up detail.

A leisurely ride in the family car to a local ice cream shop and our return home an hour later provided ample time for coals to ignite the cardboard and for the flames to do their damage. A fireman, walking back to the truck while shouldering his coiled hose, informed my father of the fire's source. My stricken face and then the tears suggested to my dad the rest of the story.

My dad was a man of few words. When those words failed and misbehavior required discipline, on more than one occasion, a leather belt to my behind spoke volumes.

My father cupped his hand behind my neck and steered me away from the crowd toward a dark corner of the yard, to a place there would be no witnesses. There was some comfort knowing what to expect.

What happened, however, was something unexpected. My father reached into his back pocket, pulled out his worn, black wallet, and handed me a five-dollar bill. What he said has stayed with me for more than forty years: "You mean much more to me than this garage."

That was it. That was all. Just nine words and five bucks. What he said was enough, but the addition of the substantive gesture was his way of backing up his affection for me.

My dad never made it past the eighth grade. He never made much money. He was not a mover and a shaker. But I believe in the five dollars he gave me that night. The monetary value aside, that gesture has reminded me over the years that life is punctuated by unexpected moments of forgiveness.

Because my dad was able to forgive me that night, I now believe in undeserved gestures of grace; in the handshake when one expects a cold shoulder; in gentle eyes when one deserves a hard stare.

I believe each of us is more than the sum total of our mistakes and failures. As my dad taught me in that single act, when we look beneath the surface of a person, we can see that even the worst of our actions do not completely represent all that we are.

I believe in the power of that five-dollar bill.

DANIEL PLASMAN has been a minister and photographer for the past thirty years, and he currently serves East Congregational United Church of Christ in Grand Rapids, Michigan. He enjoys taking pity on old houses in need of rehab, and he loves to travel with his wife to cultures where he doesn't know the language.

Nothing New Under the Sun

LAWRENCE NEWTON

I believe that what my father told me as a child is ultimately true: "There's nothing new under the sun. All matter just changes form." He introduced me to this idea at the age of eight or nine before I had any idea what it meant.

James C. Newton was a brilliant man, caught in a black skin and all the schisms that permeated black life in Washington, DC, in the 1950s and '60s. He practiced law and his clients loved him, mostly because he cared for them. He arranged adoptions for them, managed their divorces, filed their taxes, helped them buy homes, and occasionally got their errant children out of jail. He was respected universally as far as I could see. But on those rare occasions when we might dine out as a family, we were sometimes left waiting to be seated, while white patrons were ushered to readily available tables. We were just another colored family left waiting.

To further support our family, Dad worked nights delivering medications for a local pharmacy. I'd go with him sometimes. We never said much but I'd like to think he enjoyed the company as much as I did. Some evenings I'd share a problem I was having at school or around the neighborhood with him. He'd listen intently, asking a question or two until he'd heard it all. He'd say "I had a similar problem once and this is how I handled it. You know, everything will work out. There's nothing new under the sun. All matter just changes form."

Quite a few years passed before this made much sense to me. My father must have watched with a hint of humor as I stumbled into manhood, years that were full of "what-was-I-thinking" failures and gee-whiz successes. I finally learned, though, that I'm capable of being smart and stupid, strong and weak, sometimes all on the same day. And the people I've met along the way are just the same. Character and integrity were the things that mattered to Dad, and it's the same with me. As much as I resisted it, in a way, I became him. People compare me to my father. I'm proud of that. I just had to do some living to see it.

Years sailed by and, as is often the case between fathers and sons, we held one another at bay, talking at each other instead of to each other. He died in 1991 but he lived long enough to hold my infant son, Aaron, and his two sisters as well, watching them grow and me grow along with them. I wanted to be all the good things my father was to me, to pass on to them the wisdom he so patiently shared with me.

I speak with Aaron, though not as often as I should. He's working now and on his own. We'll talk a while. Sometimes Aaron confides in me about the things that trouble him. I'll listen intently, asking a question or two. He asks what I think. Then my father will step in and, in my voice, will say, "There's nothing new under the sun, all matter just changes form."

LAWRENCE NEWTON is a meeting and events manager for a major accounting firm. An alumnus of the School of Visual Arts, he continues to follow art and culture with his wife, Doris, in Washington, DC.

Respect Yourself

DAVID WESTWOOD

When I was young, my understanding of events and people was simple: things were good or bad. This made it easier for me to deal with the world around me. Then, when I became a young man, things seemed far more complicated, and instead of black and white I saw grays everywhere I looked. This made life dense with motive and decision, and more challenging to navigate. Now, as a man in middle age, and a new father, I find that my view of the world is reducing itself to the simple again.

I think this is because I'm trying to be a good parent and teach my daughter what she needs to know about life.

I naturally break complex things down into small pieces so I can explain them. And far from oversimplifying, I find this brings me back to the handful of important basics of being alive.

One of those basics is respect: respect for yourself, and respect for others. Whether it's spelling, cartwheels, piano, I teach my daughter to try. To fail feels bad, certainly, but not to have tried feels worse, because you can't respect yourself for it. And as the saying goes, if you don't respect yourself, no one else is going to do it for you.

I remember once—I must have been seven or eight—I was playing at my cousin's house with his toys. His family was better off than mine, and he had many more toys than I did. There was one in particular that I'd always wanted, and I slipped it into my pocket when he wasn't looking.

I dimly sensed, even at that age, that I would never be able to enjoy playing with the toy, nor would I ever again be able to look my cousin in the eye. I would always know I had stolen, and my opinion of myself would suffer.

His mother drove me home later, and when she dropped me off I shamefacedly pulled out the toy and gave it back. She knew, I'm sure, what had happened, but she thanked me and never spoke of it again.

I hope to help my daughter avoid similar mistakes, because I know she first has to gain self-respect before she can start truly respecting others. Then she'll be able to see and accept in them the strengths and weaknesses she already sees and accepts in herself. This, I think, is a bonding mechanism almost as powerful as love.

So I believe in respect. Because without respect there's no caring; and without caring, life is a harsh wasteland. Without respect we're all enemies, with just the occasional bridge to a friend.

I'm not perfect in this regard, far from it. But I try my best, and I respect others for trying their best in this changing world. I respect people for trying, in whatever way they can, to live according to some internal standard—to raise their children to hope, to try, and to respect.

DAVID WESTWOOD lives in Southern California. He works as a creative director at an advertising agency, is an associate coin and medal designer for the United States Mint, and in his spare time, what there is of it, he writes novels.

Gardens and Their Power to Heal

∽

ALISON VAN DIGGELEN

When my father died at the age of seventy, it was a shock that I struggled to accept, especially as I hadn't visited him for months. His death was probably as inevitable as winter rain—he endured chronic asthma his whole life in Scotland and he was weakened by tuberculosis—but it still hit me hard.

Throughout their lives together, he and my mum nurtured the kind of garden that made the neighbors pause on their evening strolls, and point and smile at the fanfare of roses and profusion of lavender by the front porch. As a kid, when I helped dad empty the grass cuttings from the rusty old lawn mower, he'd tease the passing joggers,

"Come and I'll give you some exercise—you can mow my lawn any day!"

I still treasure an image of him standing in the garden, smiling with his crooked teeth, sun glinting off his thick glasses, wearing a huge scarlet bloom in the buttonhole of his shirt.

His death and its aftermath deepened my faith in gardens, and my belief in their power to heal.

He left me an inheritance, modest in dollars, but vast in terms of his life's sacrifices. It felt wrong just to put it in the children's college funds. Instead we planted it where he might have wanted: our own backyard in California. Where a lawn once grew, there was a chaotic jumble of knee-high weeds, and beyond, a tangle of dense juniper and live oak stretching up the hill.

It took many months of effort, and it's still progressing, but now on warm summer evenings, the scent of jasmine fills the air as my kids romp around a secret path, winding through a stand of oleander. They delight in discovering new saplings and fresh blooms.

Like my dad did, I teach them to close their eyes and inhale the scent of our fragrant yellow roses, the ones that remind me most of him. Where rosemary cascades over a stone retaining wall, I can see my father lifting the skip of his tweed bonnet, scratching his bald head, and saying in his Scottish accent, "Aye, you've got yoursel' a right strong dry-staine dyke. Good, good."

Or I can see him puffing up to the deck with a view of the garden and the kids frolicking through it. "That's my girl," he'd say.

In this garden that Dad made possible, I often take time to reflect on life and am grateful for each new season. In early summer at tomato planting time, I enjoy feeling the damp clay soil between my fingers as I push the dirt firmly around the slender stalks. At harvest time, the taut flesh and rich aroma of those sweet ripe tomatoes in my hands bring me another tangible connection to home and family traditions.

During his last summer, my father wrote to me about the meaning of life—the passing of the baton, he called it, from parent to child. From growing season to growing season. I still miss his quirky humor and wheezy laugh, the twinkle in his old brown eyes, but I believe in the power of gardens to heal and help people live on in our hearts.

ALISON VAN DIGGELEN is a Silicon Valley–based journalist and host of the award-winning interview series "Fresh Dialogues." She has also interviewed writers for the Commonwealth Club of California, moderated at conferences, and taught green entrepreneurship at the University of Edinburgh Business School.

Embarrassing My Kids

ROGER MUMMERT

Dad, you dress like a geek!" "Everything you say is annoying!" "I can't stand to be seen with you!" "You're a total loser!"

Music to my ears! If I'm embarrassing my kids, I'm doing the right thing. In this age, being a parent and being cool simply aren't compatible. Rather, I believe that embarrassing my children is an inevitability—and rightfully so. I say, revel in it! It's what distinguishes us . . . from them.

Today, there is a blur in the line between children and parents. Kids are way overprogrammed. They're unable to meet the commitments they make (or we make for them) to school, religion, sports, and social events. As a belea-guered parent, I have printed out spreadsheets of their activities and shuttled them around, a half-hour late and a birthday present short. There isn't even time to discipline them when they act up. Deny them an activity, and they're happy for the break.

This blur worsens when we parents idealize the enriched lives we provide for our children (c'mon, what parent doesn't secretly want to stow away to sleep-away camp?). At the same time, kids suffer the confusion of being grown up far beyond their years: witness girls in heels and cocktail dresses at a bat mitzvah or Sweet 16 party.

Lost in this blur, I've seen other parents stop being parents and morph into junior career facilitators for their kids. Their children, fawned over and catered to, can fall into the trap of thinking they're our peers.

We never can be part of our kids' worlds, of course. And when we invade their domain—moms who dress like teen tarts, dads who sing along to Z-100—we dilute their experience and embarrass ourselves. Better to embarrass our kids than to try and pass for our kids. Our ability to mortify them empowers us!

In my case, embarrassment comes easy. I dress like a hippie who wandered into an L.L. Bean showroom. I actu-ally talk to my daughters' friends when they call. If I really want to stick it to my brand-conscious, ever-exasperated sixteen-year-old, I'll pick her up at school with cowboy yodeling on the radio full blast.

I pay for my cloddish behavior in verbal abuse, naturally, but I've never stopped being around my kids and I've never stopped being me. I won't toss them the car keys or, like some "cool parents," buy them a keg of beer for an open house. Believe me, when I'm a warts'n'all embarrassment, there's no question that I'm a dad.

Lots of parents wither in the tough years when our once-adoring kids find us repugnant. I hope that my daughters and I can reconnect sometime in the future, but for now memories sustain me.

I think back to a Father's Day card that one of my daughters gave me years ago. I can't recall her age at the time, but I remember a backwards "D" in how she wrote: "Daddy, I love you because you stay with me." And stay with my children— even as an embarrassment—I always will.

ROGER MUMMERT is a writer and lecturer. He is a contributor to the *New York Times*, where for several years he authored a monthly column on suburban life. Each year, he dons an apron to host the Latke Festival, a celebration of multiculturalism that has been profiled on CNN and NPR. A lover of cooking and culture, he has appeared many times on the Food Network, and he hosted a radio show, *Gastronomic Gossip.*

A Father's Lectures

~∽

SETH CHALMER

My father wasn't a spanker, a shouter, a poker, or a grounder. He was a lecturer. When he really got into it, I swear he channeled another dimension, some celestial debating hall in which Pericles and William James present their cases before a council of mathematicians, with the legendary Rabbi Hillel presiding.

His timing was brilliant, too. When I got a C in math, he waited to give me The Talk until we were in a moving car, so that I had nowhere to run. I could see it coming, but there was nothing to be done, except brace myself for interrogation, and prime my teenage powers of eye rolling for an epic confrontation.

Of course, it wasn't a confrontation at all, and how much easier a confrontation would have been than the reasoned interlocution that ensued. We had to dissect the consequences, and analyze the obstacles, and make a detailed plan for the future. He wouldn't quit until I understood his central points, and then he still wouldn't quit, because there were auxiliary points, alternative angles, and it turned out he felt those were actually pretty central too.

There's a story I've often told about my dad when I want to convey my admiration of him, a true story of a lecture so short it barely deserves the title. I came home from middle school and mentioned that one of the few black kids on the playground got picked on that day. I'd even heard "the 'N' word" for the first time. Dad asked if I told a teacher, and I said no, I was just glad they weren't picking on me.

"No," he said. And his voice was soft; this was different. "Do your homework" this was not. "Whenever you hear 'nigger,' hear 'dirty Jew.' Whenever you hear 'spic,' or 'fag,' or 'dyke,' hear 'dirty Jew.' And take it personally."

Those words have had an enormous impact on me. They have helped to define the person I strive to become. And so they have become the go-to story, the story of a simple lecture of justice and moral clarity.

But over the years I have come to appreciate the longer lectures too, those knots of *on-the-one-hands* and *on-the-others* I so hated as an adolescent. Sometimes the story is simple;

sometimes the lecture can be short. But nowadays, I mostly find myself shaped by convoluted auxiliary points, by caveats and nuances. Like my father, I have become a collector of alternative angles, finding sanity in interminable deliberation.

Dad doesn't care about my old math grades anymore. In truth, I'm not sure he ever did. It was the process he was pressing into my mind, the process of living as an impromptu lecture. I believe in dissecting consequences, analyzing obstacles, considering possibilities, making a plan—and doing it all now, in the moving car, without notes or preparations, whether you like it or not—because life isn't as easy as getting grounded or spanked, and there's an awful lot we have to talk through.

SETH CHALMER is a graduate student of Judaic studies and non-profit management at New York University. Previously, he helped former prisoners succeed in careers, toured the United States as a performer in *Sesame Street Live*, and served as cultural arts director of the Jewish Community Center in Dayton, Ohio.

Where the Soul of Man
Never Dies

TIM BARNES

The other day I was listening to *Prairie Home Companion*
while taking my seven-year-old son, Fergus, to soccer practice. Alison Krauss was singing an old gospel song which
happened to be one of my father's favorites, one that I
requested be sung at his funeral. I don't know if it was
because of the beautiful clarity of Alison Krauss's voice or
the sincere way in which she performed the song or maybe
all these things together, but I started listening to those
words and maybe for the first time thought about every
word of that song. *"To Canaan's Land I'm on my way where the
soul of man never dies."*

I grew up in a very conservative home in the Bible Belt South. I learned to attend church the old-fashioned way—I was forced to go. I attended every service: every Sunday morning; every Sunday night; every Wednesday night; every gospel meeting; every night of Vacation Bible School. If the doors to the church were open, my family would be there. Despite my being in church through coercion and through no exercise of free will, the indoctrination took. God was a part of my life and I believed God was good. That is, until the summer of my eleventh year.

My older brother returned from Vietnam that year and the whole extended family was overjoyed to have him back safe and unharmed. I learned about worry that year he was in Vietnam. I saw it daily in the faces of my parents. But I also learned about relief and the unburdening my parents felt when he finally came back home and was stationed in Little Rock, just two hours from home.

Then there was that summer night. Many people my age might remember that night because it was the night of the 1970 All-Star game when Pete Rose charged the catcher and scored the game-winning run for the National League. I remember it because it was the night my family received the call that my brother, while traveling back to the base in Little Rock, had been killed in a car accident. What an absurd thing to happen. What an absurdly bad thing to happen. He survived Vietnam, was stationed near home—and then, to be killed in a car accident, was to me absurd and cruel and I hated God for it. In the months and years that followed I lived in my parent's grief. For the first time in my life I saw my father cry. I wanted to help but I couldn't. And I hated God for it.

It would have been easier, I suppose, to quit believing in God. But I needed to believe in God in order to hate God. If I quit believing that would be like letting God off the hook, and I refused to do that. Over the years my hatred gradually subsided giving way, eventually, to indifference.

Then I listened to those words: *"My darkest night will turn to day and the soul of man never dies."* My father, who had died two years earlier, thirty-four years after losing his oldest son, never lost his faith. I suppose he always listened to the words of that song and believed them. Those words, I'm sure, sustained him, even through his darkest night.

So I listened. And Fergus listened. And I thought, what an absurd thing to believe. What an absurdly good thing to believe, that there could be this place, *". . . where all is peace and joy and love and the soul of man never dies."* When the song ended I turned the radio off and sat there with Fergus. After a brief quiet that followed, Fergus said, "Dad, I like that song." And I said, "I do too, Fergus. I do, too."

TIM BARNES is an attorney in Clarksville, Tennessee, and he was elected to the Tennessee State Senate in 2008. He has three children: Patrick (seventeen), Molly (thirteen), and Fergus (eleven). Mr. Barnes spends all of his time balancing the demands of his sole-practitioner law practice, legislative duties, and parenting, which can include driving hundreds of miles to see all three of his children play travel soccer.

Forgive the Rest

⁓

JULIE FEENEY

My father, James Feeney, is a first-generation Irish Catholic. His mother and father met in Boston, both having fled the potato famine. My grandfather was a roofer and an alcoholic—not the best combination, but it worked for him.

Things weren't easy for them growing up. My father shined shoes in downtown Boston and sometimes other boys beat him up and took his money. Dad isn't sure if he even graduated from high school.

My parents met when working at the same hospital; she was a medical secretary and he worked in the warehouse. With black hair, blue eyes, and a great smile, my dad got a lot of female attention and even now at seventy-six, he brags about it sometimes. What he does not like to discuss is how his mother kept my parents from getting married for years because my mother is Jewish. They finally snuck away to get married.

After they wed, things were still hard. They didn't have much money. We were forced to move several times. My parents threw things at each other when they fought and sometimes my father would take off.

Growing up, I butted heads with my father, too. He didn't understand my purple hair and my taste for hip-hop music. Once he asked me when I was going to bring a white friend home.

When I was a teenager, my father started to suffer family losses. His father, a brother, and mother all died. He became the family caretaker. He was at the hospital bed of two other siblings who died of cancer. Through all this my father began to change. He usually didn't show his feelings (other than anger), and we certainly didn't talk about them. But when his brother died, I remember seeing Dad cry.

Through his suffering, I started to be able to see the best in him. The man I once thought of as ordinary slowly became my hero. I realized he gives all that he has to the best of his ability. He has grown more tolerant and patient. Now, he even shares his emotions with us quite often. When we watch a sad movie, he joins the three women of the family for a good cry.

Recently, my father learned he has Parkinson's disease. After that diagnosis so many things make sense: the way my father walks, the way he never seems to smile anymore. The other day he told me he wished he was younger and had his stronger body back.

My response was, "Dad when you were younger you could be a real jerk. I really like the person you are now." Harsh? Maybe it is, but it's the truth. Growing up, I loved my father but I didn't often like him. Now I can do both.

Dad is marking his fiftieth year working at the warehouse, and I want him to enjoy that accomplishment. I don't want him to suffer. I want life to respect my father the way he deserves. The way I do.

I want to tell you about what I have come to believe: I believe that people can change and that we should celebrate the best that they have to give us and forgive the rest.

JULIE FEENEY is a social worker and teacher in Boston, Massachusetts. Her love and curiosity for life came from her mother, Francine, her father, James, and her sister, Margo, who always support her and encourage her to go beyond what is comfortable and safe.

His Difference Is His Strength

JAMES BUCHANAN

I believe in my son.

He is a good boy, but not like other kids. As I write, I watch him spin, then run from one corner of my small "divorced dad" apartment to another. Exhalations of energy and sound come from him. He is in his world, which is a place I cannot even begin to see or know. It is a world unto himself that I can only hope is inhabited by daydreams of soaring feats and loving friends.

My son has been diagnosed with Asperger's syndrome, which is something akin to having one's mind resting, precariously, on the doorway of autism. My son is not fully taken by his own mental world, but it is one he often retreats into.

For some time I have euphemistically called his gyrations and lurching movements the "Quincy dance." By calling it a "dance" I felt that he was unique rather than different. Then his first-grade teacher stated the obvious, that Quincy is different.

"Damn straight," I thought. "He is caring and gentle and smart and interesting and . . . and . . . and . . . so much more." But while these adjectives may be true, I would be deluding myself to think he does not face very unique challenges.

For quite a while I worried that perhaps this was my fault. That if I had been more insistent about getting his mother to a hospital as she fought obstinately to give birth at home that perhaps Quincy could be spared his dance. I worried too that the turmoil of his parents' marriage, played out before him, and our eventual divorce had irrevocably pushed him into his inner world. I worried so much that I sank into my own despair and depression. I cried at the thought that I had irrevocably scarred his life, that I had caused his life to fall to the ground even before he could live it.

Then one day he announced he wanted to join the Cub Scouts. So I signed him up and his mother bought his uniform. On the night of his first den meeting, he put on his shirt and yellow kerchief. Then he put his blue-and-yellow hat on. He said, "Look, Dad," and he stood at attention and gave me the two-fingered Cub Scout salute. He smiled broadly and every part of him exuded pride and joy.

Over the next couple of weeks we worked on his first merit badge. When he received it in front of his fellow scouts, his pride and joy ran through him to overflowing. I was never prouder of him.

It was also at that point that I realized more fully than I had before the strength of his character. I looked at this smiling little scout, and I felt the greatest sense of contentment.

Quincy will live a full life, and he will succeed. His life will be no more painful than anybody else's, and it may be more unique than most. What makes him different will make him strong.

This is what I believe. I believe in my son.

JAMES BUCHANAN is a writer living in Exeter, New Hampshire. He has published a number of essays and short stories, but takes greatest pride in his two children, Quincy and Violet. They are almost too easy to love.

The Power of Fishing

JOHNNIE BARMORE

I believe in the power of fishing. I am not an avid angler, and I'm still not sure if real flies are used in fly fishing. However when I think back on my childhood, many of my warmest and most salient memories took place on a fish bank.

I remember running, playing, exploring, and growing as the adults fished, drank beer, and talked trash to each other as B. B. King and Millie Jackson belted the blues from eight-track tape decks in deuce and a quarters and El Caminos. I remember eating the day's catch cooked outdoors on a Coleman stove. There was always plenty of hot sauce—and admonitions to be careful—with white bread on hand in case you got choked on an insidious fish bone.

One time the family went down to the pay lake with the warning, "If you don't catch a fish you'll have to walk home." Half believing this, I was delighted and relieved when I reeled in a three-pound, or was it a five-pound, no it was definitely a seven-pound catfish. After a struggle that rivaled that of Captain Ahab in *Moby Dick*, I finally got it to shore. I didn't have the nerve to take the ugly thing off the hook; luckily that was not a condition of getting a ride home. The poor fella sure was tasty, though.

As a young teen I was delighted when I reeled in seventeen white bass from the Sandusky River behind the sugar factory in Freemont, Ohio. I breathlessly told the story of my conquest to anyone who would listen. It was the last time I remember going fishing with my father. I was soon old enough to opt out, and I chose more urbane pursuits than sitting on a fish bank all day.

When my sister died unexpectedly at the age of seventeen, I remember feeling like I could not breathe. Everyone in our large family was grieving terribly. The world changed forever, like our own personal version of 9/11. Everything before that day meant something different, great or slight, the day after. I remember my father got up early the next day to go fishing—alone. It was his way of coping and everyone understood. I never saw him cry about my sister.

I often wondered if the fish did. I have a mental picture of him pouring his heart out to a wide-eyed bluegill who listened sympathetically before swimming away.

Now, in my role as a mental health therapist for children, I often take them fishing. They talk more openly when slightly preoccupied with the many little tasks it takes to fish. They are able to learn patience and skills to deal with frustration that can serve them well in school and at home. They develop courage as they tackle the daunting task of baiting their hook with a squiggly, reluctant worm. However, I think the most curative factor is that on a fish bank they are not kids with problems. They are just kids—running, playing, exploring, and healing.

JOHNNIE BARMORE lives in Cincinnati and works as a community-based mental health therapist with children. She has two daughters and a nearly human beagle. Her current projects include a book of poetry with illustrations by her daughter Phyliss, a design student at Ohio State University. Stephanie graduates high school in 2011. Princess, the dog, has plans to chase squirrels and nap.

The Greatest Thing

SCOTT KOONCE

As a boy of seventeen, with no real direction in life, I was told by my longtime girlfriend that she was pregnant. Now, the thought of catching the next bus out of town or asking the question "Do I know you?" did cross my mind momentarily. But the thought of my mother finding out I ran away from one of the greatest responsibilities I would ever face, and the thought of my child wondering who his father could be was enough to make me rethink my selfish and adolescent frame of mind. It was time for the boy to become a man. I felt as though I was jumping out of a plane without knowing for sure the parachute was packed correctly.

After weighing my limited options, I decided to graduate high school early and join the Army. Right before I shipped out to basic training, my girlfriend and I got married. It was important for me to provide a home for this child and provide everything I could for him. Having grown up watching my mother struggle to provide a good life for her kids, while at the same time tending to an alcoholic husband, I did not want my child to experience that hardship. Having a stable family life was priority number one.

As my son grew older and a daughter was born, I learned how great it was to watch them go through childhood. I also saw the changes in my wife and me as we became Mom and Dad. Although the struggles have been many, and I have the receding hairline to prove it, it has been a great lesson and a wonderful experience.

Now that I have a teenage son and a preteen daughter, I look back and see that this family has been the greatest thing to happen to me. The thing I was most afraid of has turned into the greatest experience of my life.

Now, my beautiful wife is leaving for Iraq and I cannot imagine spending that much time away from her. She has been the responsible and dedicated mother to our two kids—and to a husband who still acts like one. I have always been the one to go away, but now it is my turn to be the responsible one. So I will be the one to drive our son to his hockey games and my daughter to softball. It is time for me to handle the bills, the laundry, and the cooking—and figure out what that smell is that's coming from my son's room.

Sometimes I feel like that seventeen-year-old kid again, terrified of the responsibility and hard work. But more than that, I believe that having a family is the greatest thing to ever happen to me. It terrifies me more to think of losing them.

SCOTT KOONCE is now a manager for a Fortune 500 company in Ohio. He has two children, Mason, who is eighteen years old, and Kaitlyn, who is now sixteen.

Big Thinking

ELIZABETH SHEN

I believe that thinking small can create astonishing results.

My father, Shen Ting Wah, was a big man and a big thinker. He grew up in a small village near Nanjing in China. His family was poor and his education did not go beyond high school. By thinking big and working hard, he built a Merchant Marine business when he was in his thirties, with ships traveling to ports throughout the Pacific, trading in tons of coal, steel, iron, and other commodities. His big thinking applied to his family as well—he had eleven children.

When the Maoists came into power, my father left his entire business, ships and all, and brought as many of his family as he could to Hong Kong, where he had to start from scratch. In Shanghai, the adjective "Dah Fong"—literally "Big Direction"—is used to describe people who think big, are generous, and have their arms open wide. Keeping his eyes open and his thinking big, my father began trading again, and became a success a second time.

So, I grew up determined to be like my father, to be "Dah Fong." I decided on a career in business, intent on earning the most I could for every hour I worked. Since I'd studied music most of my life, my choices were rather limited, so I decided to work in sales. I sought out only the biggest opportunities. This tactic made me successful, and I moved up the corporate ladder quickly, always taking incredible risks, always going for bigger deals. Nothing was worth doing unless the effect and outcome were huge.

A series of events over the past few years has forced me to rethink this strategy. After the birth of my second child, a car accident, and a serious illness, I was distraught and didn't know how to continue my life. At about the same time, my father was diagnosed with cancer, and he passed away six months later.

At my father's memorial service, people showed up who were complete strangers to our family. One by one, they stood up to say a few words about my father. After retiring from business, my father had become a violin maker, and a few of the people were fellow craftsmen. Others knew him as their Chinese calligraphy teacher; some called him their Tai Chi Chuan Master. These were all people who had come a long distance to pay their last respects because my father had touched each one of them through his love, his religious faith, his generosity.

It struck me then that "Dah Fong" has to do with embracing small things with a big attitude. I had overlooked the real lesson. The reason for my father's success in life was his way of dealing with people—one person at a time—with a big heart.

Now, I'm volunteering at my son's middle school, helping motivate students and awaken the spark within each of them. And when the students ask if I'll tutor them after school, I'm delighted, and I teach them as passionately as I once went after million-dollar deals. One child at a time.

Born in Hong Kong, ELIZABETH SHEN has since made a life in the United States, and she is the proud mother of two children. Her career has included music (violin), senior management positions in telecommunications and high-tech corporations, and, more recently, working as a volunteer in local schools.

Transforming Fatherhood

ADAM KALLISH

Eight years ago, an eight-pound girl transformed my life. When my wife initially informed me that she was pregnant, the news made me happy, but my mind could not penetrate past the highly abstract concept of becoming a father. My father was a hard-working man who raised four children by himself, but he came from an age when fatherhood was an after-work activity.

My wife enrolled me in a fatherhood class at the hospital where we intended to deliver our daughter. I remember feeling awkward and wondered why I needed training to be a father. The equation was simple: the father worked, supplied resources, and was at home whenever he could be. Fatherhood was something carved out of your professional time.

The fatherhood training, held at the hospital on a cold Saturday morning, was attended by twenty other sleepy fathers-to-be—all wondering why they were enrolled as well. The content of the class focused on helping around the house, showing empathy to our wives, and changing diapers. The atmosphere of the class seemed to border on being apologetic to the men in the room now that they had to become tuned in to their home environment.

When I was in the delivery room and as my daughter was born, a new set of feelings were introduced to me. All the abstractions, training, and discussions were distilled into real feelings that were quite new and disorienting. I came to the conclusion that I wanted to spend more time with my daughter, so I resigned my position to become what many call "Mr. Mom." At first, I agreed with this term, and thought that being at home—cooking, cleaning, grocery shopping, and being at the zoo with my daughter during daylight hours—was sort of playing hooky. Compounding my feelings were the stares from confused mothers who saw me on their playgrounds during daylight hours.

Eight years later, I believe that fatherhood is going through a quiet and dramatic change that current conventional wisdom has not yet recognized. I believe that being a father means being involved with my children within a rich daily tapestry of interaction usually associated with motherhood. I know other fathers who are arranging play dates, being a room parent, waiting to pick up their kids from the bus, and listening during the tears and laughs after school.

To some, this trend may be viewed as threatening to the historical image of male attributes by being domesticated. I believe that men, in general, and specifically fathers, are more in tune with the demands of contemporary society, and we are able to be involved not just from dinner to bedtime, but from breakfast to dinner as well.

While I don't have any sons, I believe the next generation of fathers now live in a society where cooking, cleaning, laughing, crying, playing, and hugging are natural and expected items in the "job description." It has made all the difference to me.

ADAM KALLISH has been married for seventeen years and now has two middle school–age daughters. When not interacting with his family, he consults with companies about brand and user experience models intersecting applied imagination with measurable change. Mr. Kallish is known for his intensity and dry sense of humor as parent-leader of a school improvement team. He and his family live in Oak Park, Illinois.

Keep the Tempo Steady

CLAUDETTE SIKORA

When I was a little girl learning to play the piano, I practiced and Dad listened. "I think you got a little fast that time," he would often say. He was probably right. My musical goal of playing pieces as fast as my fingers were able, faster each day, ruined many a poignant melody. Yet, even so, my father's words stung. I wanted him to mind his own business. I often closed the keyboard and left in a ten-year-old huff. I did not understand then that my father was showing me he was listening—carefully. Tone-deaf, he knew little about expression or melody, but tempo was something he could understand.

My impatience with his remarks was the beginning of growing away from my friend and encourager—away from the hands that lifted me onto a kitchen chair to break eggs into pancake batter; away from flying airplanes on string; away from raising tadpoles and setting free young frogs in streams; away from carving jack-o'-lanterns in the fall and planting their seeds in spring to grow globes half my size. Dad was behind me in these exploits—and always. Had I known as a teenager when closing my bedroom door to paint on gruesome amounts of makeup that I was also closing the door on Dad; had I recognized as a young woman, lonely in a new apartment but refusing to call home, that I was forgetting to let a father know I still needed him; had I foreseen as a young mother, wanting to raise children in my own way, that I could only have benefited from the sage advice of the retired grandfather; had I realized as I grew up and away that the special closeness of a little girl and her sheltering father cannot return, then would I have slowed down a little?

If Dad was hurt by his children growing up, he never showed it. Like his advice regarding my piano playing, he kept his tempo steady. When the doctors told him how much time he had left, he asked my mother, "What will we tell the girls?" In his question was the secret of his strength: in thinking of his family first, he could put aside his own hurts, angers, and fears.

I believe that the people we love are only on loan to us, and a parent's example is a thread of immortality sewn through generations.

Sometimes, at the end of a day spent wiping noses and bottoms, pouring milk and mopping spills, and picking up Legos and Barbies and more Legos—sometimes on those evenings when I look for a quiet chair and the night's newspaper but find instead three young bodies, sticky and bickering and clamoring for a place on my lap—it's at these times when I remember Dad.

I accept the cycle of life and my part in it—that my children will one day leave me as I left my father, and I take comfort in applying and passing on my father's example. I make room for my children and hold them close.

Born in Japan and having grown up in Maryland, CLAUDETTE SIKORA is the daughter of a vivacious war bride from Normandy and a good-natured American GI. A second-generation civil servant who writes and plays music in her spare time, she is also a sister, aunt, wife, mother of two daughters and a son, and grandmother of a lively little girl. Writing the essay helped her accept the death of her father, and she hopes it will help others cope with loss.

A Lesson from My Dad

GREGORY MICHAEL ARNDT

I've held various jobs over the years, but none has had the impact on my life, on my family, on my community, as just simply being the best dad that I can be.

It's not that I'm some kind of Super-Dad. I'm your normal, average dad—the "take them to school, help with their homework, and be their baseball coach" kind of dad. Someone who's learned over the years that it's not specifically *what* you do with them; it's simply that you are with them. That's what I believe.

Maybe more important than just being there for my kids, it's also important that they know I love them. Even if I don't say it often enough, my kids know that no matter what happens, I'll always love them.

When my kids were younger, we had this little routine at bedtime. I would take them to their rooms, tuck them in bed, and whisper in their ears, "Do you want to know a secret?" They would always smile because they had heard it so many times before, but they almost always answered, "Yes, Dad, tell me a secret."

And then I would say, "I'm so happy that I'm your dad." I would look them in the eye and ask, "Do you want to know another secret?" After a nod, I'd respond, "I'm so happy that you're my little girl [or boy]." I still smile when I think about this. I wonder if they remember it too.

Those four little kids are now grown and range in age from nineteen to twenty-five. They are all happy, healthy, busy young adults. I think I did a pretty good job of teaching them how to be polite, courteous, conscientious, and to do their best. We call and visit, but I don't get to see them as much as I'd like.

I know my own dad would agree with me about fatherhood being the most important job. I learned this belief from him. I know with absolute certainty that he loved me, although I don't remember him ever saying the words. But he told me the day before he died. Although that meant a lot to me, I already knew he loved me. His actions spoke much louder than his words. He was always there—standing out behind the right field fence at my baseball games, or throwing batting practice, or asking me to hand him a wrench while he worked on my bike. He taught me how to be a man—and how to be a dad.

I believe the best job, the most important job I will ever have, is that of being a dad.

GREGORY MICHAEL ARNDT grew up in Pennsylvania, in the foothills of the Appalachians. He now loves living in Boise, Idaho, where he raised two sons, Brian and Alex, and two daughters, Lizzie and Kait. He's very proud of his children and says they are wonderful young adults, living happy lives.

Living and Loving Life

KEITH WAGNER

I believe in living. When I was nine years old, my father left for work and did not return for four months. He was a police officer in a small New Hampshire city. The phone rang shortly after his shift started and the voice on the other end told my mother that she would most likely become a widow before the night was out. My father had been run over by a semitruck while directing traffic. The accident stopped his heart and broke his back.

My mother was only twenty-nine years old at the time. She went from taking care of my sister and me to caring for my father, too. His disability was profound and long term but throughout his suffering, he would repeat the same phrase: "I am not ready to die yet." I grew up hearing this phrase over and over again. A few years later my uncle, who lived next door, took his own life just minutes after I had spoken to him. These two events changed my life but I did not realize it at the time.

My father almost had his life taken from him and wanted to live while my uncle, who had everything to live for, took his life. As I grew up, I watched my father struggle through his disabilities and health issues. It was difficult to see but I learned that he was not ready to give up. He wanted to live.

On my thirty-third birthday I received a call from a doctor who informed me that I had a terminal illness. I was devastated. My mind was consumed with thoughts of not being alive to see my daughter get married or my son graduate high school.

On the way home one night, I stopped my car on a bridge over a local lake and watched the sun set. At first I didn't notice that I was blocking traffic. Once I realized it, though, I decided I didn't care: the sunset was beautiful and I was going to watch it.

In those days my father's words came back to me: I am not ready to die yet. I decided I was going to really live what little life I had left. My relationships with people started to change. I began to tell people what I really thought.

I held my children and my wife in a way that I had not done before. I wanted to live each day as if it were my last.

One month later I received another call from the doctor who told me that a terrible mistake had been made and that the test was wrong. I was fine. I was thrilled to get this news but soon realized that my life had changed forever. Despite my terminal diagnosis I was having too much fun.

Now ten years later, my days are consumed with living. I go to every one of my daughter's high school basketball games. I am the loudest and most positive one in the stands. My son's Little League team challenged me to dye my hair pink if they made a double play in the next game. They did it and I did it. When it happened again, the players wanted green hair. They got it. I am living. I have an amazing sense of freedom. I am loving life.

A month ago my father had a heart attack. Things looked grim and I flew home to be with him. When I arrived, he was surprised to see me. He said, "What are you doing here? I'm not ready to die yet."

I smiled, hugged him, and told him that I loved him.

KEITH WAGNER lives in The Woodlands, Texas, with his wife, Joanne, and two children, Victoria (Tori) and Kyle. He owns and operates his own insurance agency. Mr. Wagner has written a top-ten list of things to do before he dies. He is on number four.

The Best Education in the World

JEFF SLOAN

This I Believe began for me on July 30, 1994, at about 6:30 P.M. when the maternity nurse at St. Joseph Hospital in Denver handed me my just-delivered, freshly bundled, firstborn son. My wife, Sheila, lay on the bed next to me, exhausted after a very long and difficult labor and delivery. For what seemed like and was a long time I simply sat with Thomas cradled between my arms and gazed down at him as he too dozed after his twelve-hour arrival.

I marveled at the life and energy we'd created in this miniature person and recall a swirl of fear, fatigue, and fascination as I pondered my new situation. I wondered if I was really ready for the immense responsibility I held in my hands, and then realized that I didn't have a choice.

More than sixteen years later, and now the father of three boys, I find myself thinking often about how being a father has molded and shaped my beliefs and restructured my priorities. Along the way, I've developed a few core beliefs.

I believe in giving our kids choices: my wife and I hold ultimate authority in the family, but whenever possible we give our kids the power to choose how they will guide themselves and contribute to the functioning of our home and family. Do you want to scrub the toilets or mop the halls? Do you want to take a bath or a shower? Broccoli or cauliflower with dinner?

I believe the entire family should come together at the end of every day for a meal at a table; it's easy, between practices, music lessons, and meetings to let this belief go, but there is at the dinner table an irreplaceable reconnection of family, where stories and experiences of the day are shared and explored.

I believe that a father is not a babysitter—when I am with the boys and my wife is not with us, I am first their father, and that relationship is paramount. I'm not "watching the kids" in my wife's absence, and I am not the stand-in parental unit. Being my boys' father entitles me to all of the benefits and responsibilities of the job, all of the time.

I believe in the power of Legos. I believe in reading aloud. I believe in running around in the yard and throwing baseballs with my kids. I believe that a long family vacation in one vehicle builds character. I believe my kids should do chores and earn an allowance for the effort. I believe in pancakes made from scratch on a Saturday morning and the reading of comics on a Sunday morning. I believe in telling my boys stories, and I believe our kids have the most fun when the TV is off. I believe in tucking the kids into bed every night, and I believe in waking them in the morning.

And after all these years I believe I still have a lot to learn as a father, but it's the best education in the world.

JEFF SLOAN is editor of a technical magazine serving the composites manufacturing industry. In his modest spare time he coaches and plays soccer, rides his bike, loves to cook, and bakes a mean loaf of bread. He lives in Pueblo West, Colorado, with his wife, Sheila, and sons, Thomas, Jacob, and Isaac.

What It Takes

SHELBY CROWLEY

My eyes are blue and his are green, but that's okay, we're not related. But when you look past the difference in our eyes, the shape of our noses, and the tone of our skin, you can see a definite resemblance. I hold my head up high with confidence like he taught me. I speak my mind, and I have to know "why"—these characteristics are a product of his sacrificed time with me.

Going back and forth between my mother's and father's house took some getting used to, but the worst part was thinking their divorce was my fault. That thought haunted me year after year, but the man who entered my life when I was only four years old changed my entire outlook on the situation. He gradually taught me that it wasn't my fault and that the world is a strange place but thank God it's only temporary.

He is six foot two and as rough as his callused hands, but his heart is tender like warm butter on hot breakfast pancakes. He is the man who gave me baths and tucked me in at night, and he was also the man who whipped my tail when it was necessary. This man is the one who drove me to school dances and waited up until I came home with a mouthful of stories. He was the one who listened intently and never complained, with an understanding smile.

This man was the one who bought me my first truck and intimidated my first boyfriend who just so happened to be a brave senior who asked me to prom. This man gave me the advice I didn't want to hear, but I never listened and still after that boy ripped out my heart and I felt like I was dying, he was the one who told me, "Honey your heart is still there because I would never let some boy run off with something so precious."

He thought he was ten feet tall and bulletproof, and I won't lie, I thought so too. He is, was, and will always be my hero. His name is not on my birth certificate and we don't share the same DNA, but who is to say that he can't be my dad? Who will tell me that the person who raised me and taught me right from wrong is not my dad? Who?

He is a man who stood up and took responsibility for four children who weren't even his. He is mighty and brave. He is my dad, the man I believe in. I believe that any man can become a father, but it takes a real man to become a dad.

SHELBY CROWLEY is a high school senior, graduating in the top quarter of her senior class. She plans to attend college to learn to become a speech pathologist. She is passionate about music and lives to see people smile. She wants to thank her stepfather for giving her the chance to have a better life, and she hopes he is proud of her.

With Brown Shoes to Match

$\sim$

BRIAN M. WISE

My father calls me his storyteller. From the age of five to the age of eighteen, he said everything that came out of my mouth was a story, ranging from the early childhood dreams about flying over mountains to the lies you tell your parents when you get caught sneaking out of bed at midnight to go sit by the river with your friends.

My father has always worked in an unpoetic world of microscopes and backwash filters with the foundation of life. For thirty years, he presided over a lime-green building perched on a hill above the McKenzie River that cleans and pumps water to the citizens of Eugene, Oregon. He has always been good at what he does.

Dad's storytelling was limited to the ways and means of protozoa and bacteria. I remember counting *E. coli* under a microscope for a penny a petri dish for my first allowance, and explaining to my kindergarten class what *Giardia* does to a child's body. (This was also the cause of my father's very first parent-teacher conference.) Road trips involved carrying our own titration kits and testing water at hotel taps, boiling all camping water, and freezing our own. I knew the plastic leech rates of a water bottle in 1986. Literacy in the ways of water came purely by osmosis.

When I found out my dad was one of the most published men in his profession, with one of the most comprehensive fields of knowledge in water quality in the nation, I was confused. My father? The stumbling, taste-challenged microbiologist who still cannot tell the difference between grapefruit juice and apple juice? The semigeeky man I knew growing up who always wore white short-sleeved shirts and pants to work, with brown shoes to match?

Then I looked at the things he had surrounded himself with in his life. The river stones in his study, the fountains, the aquariums—even the blues and grays and greens of his favorite clothes and his cars. Water surrounds him. Every day he gets up early, puts on a white shirt and slacks and brown shoes to match, and he goes to make water clean and affordable. When he heard people bottled his water from the tap and sold it, he shrugged, smiled a little, and called it a compliment. He may not always do the job for the rest of his life, or always be in a green building with white trim, but water is who he is. He is great, and I am the product of that greatness.

I stopped wondering long ago what it would be like to be the son of a great painter or the child of a Nobel laureate. I am the son of a water man—maybe the best one in the world. I may not reach fame or fortune, but if I can find something of his skill, compassion, and art in my work, I believe that is greatness enough for me.

BRIAN M. WISE is a technical documentation developer, a writer specializing in unpublished fiction, and a community arts organizer living in the Seattle area. He lives with his wife, Tara, and on occasion, he trades stories—true or not—with his father, Douglas Wise. They both still carry portable titration kits.

Forever in Love

~⌒~

GREG WEES

It used to be when people spoke of heaven, I could conjure up no working version of the place apart from the usual caricature of white clouds, pearly gates, and feathery wings on the backs of beatific angels—I could not conceive of a spiritual realm outside of earthly existence. This was because, as a realist, I had no evidence, no facts to work with.

Then the other day my young daughter asked me, in her point-blank way, "Do you believe in heaven?" Before I knew her, I might have quickly answered that question. But when she asked, and as I looked into her eight-year-old eyes, I decided not to be evasive just to soothe her imagination.

"You know I love you, don't you?" I asked her.

"Yes," she said.

"And I know I love you. I think that is what heaven is," I told her. "It's the place where we know love."

I don't think that satisfied her, but it satisfied me. The idea occurred as a new realization and remains with me. I believe that heaven is the name we give to the idea of shared love among human families.

I spent my young adulthood denying the possibility of any reality outside of the confines of my body and my physical environment, taking my lessons about life from the surface elements of existence—the death, destruction, greed, indifference, hatred, and hypocrisy that crowd the pages of our book of days. Becoming a student of history only made things worse. Discovering that humanity has been refining the methods of inhumanity in war and empire-building since our earliest societies was an object lesson in pessimism. It became easy to believe that all goodness and all good people are merely the lighter shades of a darker truth about humankind.

But something happened to change this belief. I experienced the unselfish love of marriage, and together my wife and I nurtured the shared love of family. The moment my daughter was born, my education in pessimism was swept away by the stern insistence in her eyes. In place of the world I had lived in, a new world was created. It was a world of innocence, of purity, a world unburdened of the baggage of the past, untainted by any imagined original sin.

Regina arrived on a rainy morning in June. Later that day, as I looked out the hospital window, the clouds parted, and I saw a strange new beauty in the shining black streets, the bright stoplights, the bobbing umbrellas, the broad fresh sky. It felt as if all things were new, and I was seeing this city for the first time. I suddenly knew that the possibilities of life greatly outweigh its trials and disappointments. More important, I finally knew love of a kind I had never believed could exist, an immortal love embodied in a new family inheriting a new world, a world that no longer lacked a place to call heaven.

GREG WEES is a writer and teacher. He lives in Omaha, Nebraska, with his wife, Coreen, and daughter, Regina.

My Father, Christ

WHITNEY ALT

I find it ironic my father is named Christ. Though it was a simple error in my grandmother's penmanship, it almost seems to fit his character. He is caring, compassionate, and strong—just like Jesus. Inside his big, tough body is the kindest heart that I will ever know. I have been blessed to have such a great father.

Dad prefers to go by the name Chris. He stands at five-foot-seven and is built muscularly; even his deep brown eyes are full of strength. He has been my family's rock since he took full responsibility for us kids after it became apparent my mother had a gambling problem and disappeared to bingo halls and the casino on a regular basis.

Dad did everything for us. He would work an eleven-hour day, then sit in on one of our sports practices, feed us dinner, help us with the little math he could, and then put us to bed. On more than one occasion, he has sold a race car or motorcycle to pay for a retainer, football cleats, or a clarinet. He even bought some maxi-pads for me on the day I became a woman.

In March of 2008 my Dad suffered a massive heart attack. At the age of forty-nine—the same age his father died from a massive heart attack—life caught up to him. It is an honest miracle that he's still alive. EMS had to defibrillate him eighteen times.

About a week after his heart attack, when he was still in the hospital, he grabbed my hand, and said softly, "I'm scared." It was at that point I learned the true strength my father had—and he has instilled that same strength in me.

I believe that being strong is about more than endurance or physical strength. It's about being there for someone when they need you. Just like my father had always been there for us, now I had to be strong for him. There, in the hospital, when I really just wanted to start sobbing, I held my composure and told my dad, "Don't be scared. Everything is going to be okay."

My father had lived his life under the pretense that he had to be strong for everyone else, and then he didn't have enough strength left for himself. Now, my dad doesn't work seventy hours a week anymore. He doesn't race cars or ride motorcycles either. These days you will find him leading the pit crew for my brother and cruising on his ATV. He works his normal forty hours, goes home to spend time with his family, and cherishes every minute with the grand-babies he almost never met.

I give my dad full credit for the way I turned out, and I thank him for teaching me how to be strong.

WHITNEY ALT lives in Howell, Michigan, where she is currently studying criminal justice at Schoolcraft College. She and her husband, James, love playing indoor soccer and spending time with their very spoiled beagles. Ms. Alt considers family to be the most important thing in her life.

Making Choices That
Make Me Smile

CHRISTOPHER SWIECKI

I believe you should smile going to work and smile coming home from work. I clearly remember learning this lesson from my father when I was a young boy, not yet considering a career or a family. He doesn't remember giving me this advice, but I have seen him live it.

Smiling on the way to work shows that you enjoy your job. You feel satisfied, appreciated, and, despite the inevitable daily grind, you're having fun. Work is not always what you do to make a living. It can be staying home with the children, a retirement passion, or any daily endeavor. Having a goal keeps you engaged in life.

Smiling on the way home from work is evidence that you enjoy your family. You are excited to see your spouse, your children, the pets. You enjoy hearing the day's events, helping with homework, eating dinner together, and settling into the rhythm of life at home.

My father worked as a large- and small-animal veterinarian in a small Wisconsin town. He enjoyed the characters he met on the dairy farms. He would smirk telling us stories of odd pets and their owners. It was clear he enjoyed his job.

In my teenage years, he gave up the large-animal half of his practice. It was hard to see all my basketball games with emergency calls early in the morning and late in the evening, which is when the farmers checked on the cattle. He said it was time to scale back. I know better; he was not smiling as much, so he made a change.

When he retired, his daily "work" was gone. He's not a golfer or a tennis player. He didn't have a daily activity to make him smile. Over the next few years, he talked my mother into joining the Peace Corps, took care of his ailing father, took up woodcarving, decided to learn Spanish, and took part in short medical mission trips. It took a few years, but he is back to smiling when going to work.

I have always tried to live by his example. I chose the rigorous road of attending a military academy. The challenge made me smile. I chose to be a surgeon, a career I enjoy despite the long hours, the late night calls, and the heartaches. And I also smile on my way back home. I found the love of my life, have three beautiful daughters, and can't wait each day to get home to them. Just the thought of the three bouncy blonde girls running up to hug me, yelling "Daddy, you're home!" makes me smile.

I believe that making choices that make me smile on the way to work and smile on the way home creates a life that is rich, full, meaningful, and—most of all—fun.

CHRISTOPHER (KIT) SWIECKI is a general surgeon who recently left the Army after fifteen years and moved back to Wisconsin. His wife of eleven years, Dee Dee, and his three daughters, Mackenzie, Brooke, and Claire, are always on the hunt for new adventures to make them smile.

The Measure of a Man

∽

SUSAN CRAMER

For a few years after my stepfather died, I walked through life with the image of him saying good-bye to my young son, a beloved grandchild. It brought on unexpected bouts of tears, usually when it was least convenient and most embarrassing. I was shocked at how much I missed him.

He married my widowed mother long after I left home. In the beginning, I was grateful that she had found someone who would take over worrying about her, but I secretly thought of him as her intellectual inferior. I am a snob, not an idiot, so I eventually grew to love him as he deserved, but it wasn't until after his death that I began to admire him as well.

His name was Kermit and he was completely comfortable sharing his name with the world's most famous frog. An ex-Marine and opera buff, he was a man who defied stereotypes. His closest friends included a college professor, a tire salesman, a thoracic surgeon, and a maintenance man. He accepted people as they were, and was, in turn, exactly who he seemed to be. He was, according to his professor friend, "A man without an agenda."

In his fifties, he became an instructor with what was then called the Disabled Skier Program. Winter afternoons would find him sporting his signature knickers and snowflake knee socks, guiding a blind girl down the slope or flying down the mountain in the wake of a one-legged skier, yodeling badly at maximum volume. When complimented on his service to others, he would say only that he loved to go fast. But I learned to admire the elegance with which he combined purpose and passion.

He came to Ohio to say good-bye the winter before he died. We pretended that it was a regular visit, although we all knew that he and my mother never left the mountain during ski season. Except for the added layers of clothing he wore because the radiation treatments made him constantly cold, he was as he'd always been, smacking his lips over a few bites of a candy bar and wrapping up the rest for later, and reading to the bottom of the menu even after ordering just to make sure he hadn't missed anything wonderful. Together, we watched the news, visited a local museum, went out for dinner. The day they left, we had his favorite breakfast. He ate each one of his tiny pancakes with a different flavored dollop of syrup.

"Grandpa, how come you eat your pancakes like that? Don't you have a favorite?"

"I got so many favorites I can never pick one. There's alotta great stuff out there, chief."

I have come to believe in my stepfather's formula for a rich and happy life: be individual enough to wear clothing that will embarrass your children. Be open to experiencing everything life has to offer from six different flavors of pancake syrup to a paddle boat cruise on the Mississippi. And have the grace to help someone else fly down the mountainside.

It seems to me that the measure of a man is not the car in which he drives through life, but the size of the hole left behind when he leaves it. I believe that greatness can be accomplished through small as well as monumental deeds, and that average people—like my stepfather—can make a big difference in small ways.

SUSAN CRAMER runs *Power of the Pen,* her middle school's creative writing club. Following Kermit's example, she has happily served as president of the Board of Trustees of the Granville Public Library for many years. Ms. Cramer lives in Ohio with her husband, and they have two almost perfect children.

Little Acts of Goodness

HOWARD MILLER

Shakespeare once wrote: "The evil that men do lives after them; the good is oft interred with their bones." With all due respect to the Bard, I believe that the good that people do lives on as well.

Thirteen years ago, at the age of eighty-one, my dad died quietly in his kitchen while making his morning coffee. My dad was an average guy and a wonderful dad. Soon after his death, I would learn something that would change how I was to remember him and how I would live the rest of my life.

The story begins in the 1950s when I was ten. My entire life was the New York Yankees. On rare and exuberant

sions, Dad and I would head for Yankee Stadium for a double header.

Down the street from me—and a world apart—lived another Yankee fan, Stanley. Stanley was from a family of six who lived in a converted garage. His dad was blind, his mom was overworked yet always had a warm smile, and Stanley was always in and out of trouble. One day he surprised everyone by winning an essay contest, and the prize was tickets to a Yankees game. Because none of his family members could take him to the game, Stanley began asking every adult he knew: his teachers, his principal, his priest. No takers. When I mentioned Stanley's quandary to my dad, he said, "Let's do it."

Mind you, Stanley and I were not close. We were in the same grade, and once or twice we might have played catch or sat in his garage loft to study his autograph collection. But mostly we ignored each other. Yet we went to that game.

Soon after arriving at the stadium, Stanley set off on his own to explore. My dad loved Stanley's spirit. "Is that Stanley over there in the bleachers?" It was. Near the end of the game, when we wondered if Yankee Stadium had swallowed Stanley alive, we heard the stadium announcer summon security to the Yankees dugout. Stanley was leaning over the roof asking players for autographs. After reuniting with Stanley at the stadium office, we rode the elevated subway back up to the Bronx, exhausted and happy.

And I forgot about Stanley and that day for the next forty years, until the evening of my dad's funeral.

The director entered the parlor and whispered that I had a phone call. It was Stanley. He had seen notice of my dad's death and wanted to pay his respects. He recalled vividly that Saturday forty years ago, a day that would remain with him through juvenile detention and longer incarcerations. He told me, "Your dad believed in me when no one else would." He said he'd had some tough times, but eventually finished college and earned a master's degree in social work. "Now I counsel kids who are in trouble like I was. Every day I try to do for someone what your dad did for me."

I hung up and sat there, my dad lying in the next room—an average guy, a wonderful dad, and someone who taught me the power of those little acts of goodness that live on after us.

Following a twenty-five-year career as a summer camp director, HOWARD MILLER retired to Stuart Country Day School in Princeton, New Jersey, to fulfill a dream as a science teacher. Deeper into his retirement now, he plans to help young people catch fire for science in his new home of Charlottesville, Virginia.

Leaving Work to Gaze at Sunsets

LAURIE GRANIERI

I believe in leaving work at five o'clock.

In a nation that operates on a staunch Protestant work ethic, this belief could be considered radical. Working only forty hours a week? I just don't know many people who punch out at five o'clock anymore. It seems downright quaint, like pocket watches and shoe shines.

My father tried to teach me the importance of hard work, long hours, and dedication to a career. But then there are the things he taught me unintentionally, like when he arrived home from work for the last time and crawled up the stairs.

My father, a self-employed sales trainer, was that ⸱⸱⸱ that tired. His body was wracked with liver cancer, and ⸱⸱⸱ suffered the effects of a diabetic ulcer. Still, he insisted on traveling to honor his commitment to give a seminar. He probably earned a lot of money that day, and he paid the price: He returned to the hospital soon after and was dead within three months, at age fifty-eight.

It's been ten years since I saw my father come home that night and since then, I've thought a lot about work. I've decided something: I will never crawl up the stairs. As much as I love my job as a newspaper reporter, I will never work myself into the ground, literally or figuratively.

The idea of leaving work at work didn't come easily to me. After all, I am my father's daughter. In college, I wasn't going to keg parties in a frat basement; I was the girl who lingered on the library steps each morning, waiting for the doors to open. I even dreamt about schoolwork.

My dad once told me he was unable to just gaze at a sunset; he had to be doing something as he looked at it—writing, reading, playing chess. You could say he was a success: he was a published author, an accomplished musician, fluent in German and the American Sign Language. That's an impressive list, but here's the thing: I want to gaze at sunsets. I don't want to meet a deadline during them or be writing a column at the same time, or glance at them over the top of a book.

. his raises the question: If I leave work at five o' clock watch the sunset, what are the consequences? Do I risk not reaching the top of my profession? Maybe, because honestly, knocking off after eight hours probably won't earn me the corner office or the lucrative promotion.

But, hey, leaving work at five o' clock means I eat dinner with my family. I get to hop on my bike and pedal through the streets of my hometown as the shadows lengthen and the traffic thins.

And I get to take in a lot of sunsets. That's got to be worth something.

LAURIE GRANIERI left newspaper reporting in October 2009 to become the director of public relations at Rutgers University's Mason Gross School of the Arts in New Brunswick, New Jersey. She grew up in a house full of books. Her father urged her to "write every day," and she's doing her best to follow his advice. Ms. Granieri lives in Milltown, New Jersey.

A Stack of Rocks

∽

RON WOOLLEY

I believe that making a stack of rocks by the sea keeps my father's memory alive.

Twenty-odd years ago when I warned my Catholic parents that I was an atheist, my father was particularly concerned. He told me it was important to believe in something. Although I didn't fully understand it at the time, he was a man who had faced down more than his share of demons, and he spoke with the wisdom of experience. As a typically defiant adolescent I refused to accept my father's advice, which I perceived as more of a mandate, but I did think about it a lot over the years.

My mother, my brothers, and I were at my father's hospital bedside when he died three years ago. To see a man who had once been a champion diver and a man of action suffer paralysis and death over three days was predictably horrible. But as the heart monitor went flat, my father's face took on a majestic aspect like the death mask of Agamemnon.

What we did after my father died was illegal; nonetheless, it was the right thing to do. We released his ashes in the Gulf of Mexico off the coast of southern Florida where he regularly swam. My mother scooped his ashes out of a small wooden box with a white seashell found on the beach. Spontaneously, my brothers and I jumped into the water. It might have seemed like some sort of New Age ritual, but we were in the midst of a straight-laced Florida retirement community.

Some time ago I heard a piece on the radio about the air that Julius Caesar breathed. Apparently there is a 98.2 percent chance that the air I just inhaled contained one of the molecules in Caesar's last breath. Although I was neither sure of the math behind it, nor particularly excited about the prospect of sharing Caesar's breath, I couldn't shake the concept. Like my father's advice from years before, I didn't really understand it, but I reflected on it a lot.

Today, I live in New England across the street from the Atlantic Ocean, and I try to swim in the saltwater every chance I get. Swimming has always brought me a tremendous joy, but since my father's death the experience has become transcendent. Now when my face first splashes under the water I am immediately reminded of two things: Caesar's last breath and my father's ashes. My math may be fudged, but if Caesar's breath can get around, I figure my father's ashes can make it from south Florida to the Massachusetts Bay. And as I move through the water I believe that my father is there in some way.

Each time I trudge out of the water onto the rocky shore, I kneel down and stack some rocks atop one another. Sometimes it's just three teetering stones that probably get knocked over before I even get home. Other times it's an elaborate piece of architecture that survives a few high tides. My father doesn't have a gravestone, because he doesn't have a grave. He has a pile of rocks on the shore because he taught me how to swim and how to believe in something.

RON WOOLLEY lives in Cohasset, Massachusetts, with his family. He bikes to nearby Hingham where he teaches world history and economics at the high school. He is currently helping his two sons learn to swim.

When Angels Miss

D. JOHN DYBEN

Like all little children, my seven-and-a-half-year-old daughter gets scared sometimes when she is trying to go to sleep. If the wind is howling just right or she happened to see something scary on TV, her imagination can begin working overtime and she may see a figure in the shadows or hear the sound of a sinister laugh in the wind.

This past Monday was one such night. Shortly after putting her to bed, she came into my room crying that she was scared. She said she was sure she heard the sound of a bad guy laughing and she was petrified that someone was going to get all of us. Her tears cut my heart, as they always do, and I held my daughter tight and assured her that I would not let anything happen to her. I walked her back into her room and lay down beside her to continue to assure her that all was well and I would keep her safe.

"Yes I know you will always protect me, Daddy, but what about when you go to sleep?" she asked.

I think I may have begun to get a little nervous myself at this point.

"Sweetheart," I replied, "there are great big angels all around this house, and they never sleep. They are here just to protect us. They can stop any bad guy from getting in here, so you can sleep well knowing they're around."

A brilliant and irrefutable answer, if I do say so myself!

"But, Daddy, what about when the angels miss? I mean like when kids are kidnapped or robbers do break into people's houses or like that great big tsunami that killed all of those people—what about those times? I mean, at least some of those people had to have had angels too, right?"

Ya know, sometimes kids have a really sneaky way of interrupting perfectly comfortable theology.

"How do I get out of this one?" I wondered. And then it struck me—when did I start avoiding these questions? When did I begin to put blinders on my beliefs so as not to consider the most obvious questions and problems of our existence? I mean, I deal with problems and traumas and ragedies every day—and I am taken aback by this simple question.

Ironically, I think I may have started ignoring these questions a bit more when my daughter and I began talking a few years ago—when she started to ask questions. And this question brought light to a simple trap that I have fallen into in my own thinking: the belief that I must have answers that will make her feel good. I don't really know where it comes from, but there it is.

And so I considered her question and realized there is no perfect answer. I realized that making my daughter feel good was not my highest call. And so I drew my breath and simply stated, "I don't know, sweetheart."

And so I lay there a little longer, I held her a little tighter, and I went back to my original answer, "I am with you."

D. JOHN DYBEN is a therapist, educator, and pastor. He currently serves as the clinical director of a treatment center and teaches at a state college. He is an avid writer and musician who loves being a father more than anything in the world. Mr. Dyben lives with his wife and two children in South Florida.

How to Write Your Own
This I Believe Essay

We invite you to contribute to this project by writing and submitting your own statement of personal belief. We understand how challenging this is—it requires such intimacy that you may find it difficult to begin. To guide you through this process, we offer these suggestions:

Tell a story. Be specific. Take your belief out of the ether and ground it in the events of your life. Your story need not be heartwarming or gut-wrenching—it can even be funny—but it should be real. Consider moments when your belief was formed, tested, or changed. Make sure your story ties to the essence of your daily life philosophy and to the shaping of your beliefs.

Be brief. Your statement should be between 350 and 500 words. The shorter length forces you to focus on the belief that is central to your life.

Name your belief. If you can't name it in a sentence or two, your essay might not be about belief. Rather than writing a list, consider focusing on one core belief.

Be positive. Say what you do believe, not what you don't believe. Avoid statements of religious dogma, preaching, or editorializing.

Be personal. Make your essay about you; speak in the first person. Try reading your essay aloud to yourself several times, and each time edit it and simplify it until you find the words, tone, and story that truly echo your belief and the way you speak.

Please submit your completed essay to the *This I Believe* project by visiting the Web site, www.thisibelieve.org. We are eager for your contribution.

ACKNOWLEDGMENTS

First, and most important, we wish to offer our deepest thanks to the essayists who contributed their personal statements to this book. We honor their willingness to explore and express the things that matter most and to share their stories in this collection.

In reviving *This I Believe* we are forever grateful to Casey Murrow, Keith Wheelock, and Margot Wheelock Schlegel, the children of *This I Believe* creators Edward R. Murrow and Ward Wheelock. Our project continues to be guided by Edward R. Murrow and his team, which preceded us in the 1950s: Gladys Chang Hardy, Reny Hill, Donald J.

Merwin, Edward P. Morgan, Raymond Swing, and Ward Wheelock.

Very special thanks go to Atlantic Public Media, Inc., in Woods Hole, Massachusetts, where many of these essays were first reviewed. Several essays in this collection were originally broadcast on NPR, and we are thankful to Jay Allison and Viki Merrick for their contribution in editing and producing these essays: "Life Is Wonderfully Ridiculous," "The Choice to Do It Over Again," "Work Is a Blessing," "The Give and Take of Grief," "I Am Capable of More Than I Think I Am," and "Leaving Work to Gaze at Sunsets."

For their insightful guidance and enthusiastic assistance, we are so very grateful for our This I Believe, Inc., board of directors: Marty Bollinger, John Y. Brown III, Jerry Howe, David Langstaff, Lynn Amato Madonna, and Declan Murphy.

Our current on-air home is *The Bob Edwards Show* on Sirius XM Satellite Radio and *Bob Edwards Weekend* on Public Radio International. Our sincerest thanks go to Bob Edwards and his wonderful staff: Steve Lickteig, Geoffrey Redick, Ed McNulty, Ariana Pekary, Shelley Tillman, Dan Bloom, Andy Kubis, Chad Campbell, and Cristy Meiners. At Sirius XM, we thank Jeremy Coleman, Frank Raphael, and Kevin Straley.

We also want to express our gratitude to everyone at NPR, which aired our radio series for four years, especially Jay Kernis,

Stacey Foxwell, and Robert Spier, who were passionate and steadfast supporters.

Without our funders, our project simply would not be possible. *This I Believe* received the first faithful leap of funding from the Corporation for Public Broadcasting. Over the years, we have also received corporate underwriting from Farmers Insurance, Capella University, Prudential Retirement, E.ON US, and, most recently, Kellogg's Corn Flakes. In addition, we have received grants from the Righteous Persons Foundation and the Prudential Foundation. We are also extremely grateful for donations from individuals who support our programming and mission.

The comprehensive Web site for *This I Believe* (thisibelieve .org) was built by Dennis Whiteman at Fastpipe Media, Inc., and was designed by the folks at LeapFrog Interactive with help from Chris Enander of TBD Design. Our iPhone app was cocreated by Dennis along with Wayne Walrath at Acme Technologies.

The creation of this book was immeasurably aided by our agent, Andrew Blauner, of Blauner Books Literary Agency. We are so fortunate to have had his able services and his unwavering support.

Our publisher, John Wiley & Sons, has been tremendously supportive of our recent publishing activities. We are obliged to editor Alan Rinzler and his team at Wiley's Jossey-Bass imprint for seeing the potential in this book

.d for putting time and care into its creation. We are deeply grateful for the talents of Nana Twumasi, Carol Hartland, Donna Cohn, and Susan Geraghty in helping bring this book to life.

And, finally, we thank the thousands of individuals who have accepted our invitation to write and share their own personal statements of belief. This book contains but a fraction of the many thoughtful and inspiring essays that have been submitted to our project, and we are grateful for them all. We invite you to join this group by writing your own *This I Believe* essay and submitting it to us via our Web site, thisibelieve.org. You will find instructions in the Appendix of this book on how to do so.